Housing in the Rhondda

1800–1940

Malcolm J. Fisk

MERTON PRIORY PRESS

Published by Merton Priory Press Ltd
7 Nant Fawr Road, Cardiff CF2 6JQ

First published 1996

ISBN 1 898937 11 7

© Malcolm J. Fisk 1996

Dedication. This book is dedicated to the Evans family (Barbara, Marion, Bobby and Stephen) and Cyril Heal, without whom I might never have come to know and love the Rhondda. MJF

Printed by Hillman Printers (Frome) Ltd
Handlemaker Road, Marston Trading Estate
Frome, Somerset BA11 4RW

Contents

	List of Figures and Plates	4
	Acknowledgements	6
1	Introduction	7
2	The Pre-Industrial Period	11
3	The Early Period of Industrial and Housing Development 1840–79	19
4	The Colliery Owners	39
5	Building Clubs	48
6	Private Developers, Investors and Other Agencies of Housing Provision	57
7	Water, Sanitation and Public Health	75
8	The Decline of the Private Sector	83
9	Housing Reform and the Emergence of Council Housing	93
10	Conclusions	112
	Appendices	119
	Bibliography	123
	Index	126

List of Plates and Figures

Plates

1	Tyntyla Farm, Ystrad	69
2	Long Row, Blaenllechau	69
3	Glanselsig Terrace, Blaenycwm	70
4	Caroline Street, Blaenrhondda	70
5	Colliery houses at Tylorstown	71
6	Concrete Houses, Dinas	71
7	Baptist Square, Blaenllechau	72
8	Llyn Crescent, Ferndale	72
9	Sherwood Street, Llwynypia	73
10	Fernhill Garden Suburb, Blaenrhondda	73
11	Eileen Place, Treherbert	74
12	Highfield, Maerdy	74

Figures

2.1	Tŷ Du, Cymmer	13
2.2	Typical cottage farm	15
2.3	Tyntyla Farm, Ystrad	17
3.1	28 High Street, Cymmer	21
3.2	Penygefnen, Dinas	22
3.3	32 Mary Street, Porth	26
3.4	8 Railway Terrace, Cwmparc	27
3.5	4 Glanselsig Terrace, Blaenycwm	28
3.6	19 Ton Row, Ton Pentre	29
3.7	3 Holyrood Terrace, Llwynypia	31
3.8	Houses planned for Brynwyndham Village, Treherbert	34
4.1	Caroline Street, Blaenrhondda	41
4.2	5 East Road, Tylorstown	43
4.3	31 Hillside Terrace, Wattstown	44
4.4	4 Nythbrân Terrace, Llwyncelyn	46

5.1	3 Redfield Street, Ystrad	52
5.2	8 Llyn Crescent, Ferndale	54
6.1	138 Gelli Road, Gelli	60
6.2	10 Brown Street, Ferndale	61
6.3	43 Sherwood Street, Llwynypia	62
6.4	Under 35 Commercial Street, Blaenllechau	64
6.5	Under 37 Marion Street, Clydach Vale	65
6.6	137 Miskin Road, Trealaw	66
9.1	37 Bransby Street, Penygraig	98
9.2	85 Pleasant View, Wattstown	102
9.3	20 Church Street, Llwynypia	108

Abbreviations used in Footnotes

GRO   Glamorgan Record Office, Cardiff.

RMOH   Report of the Medical Officer of Health for the year indicated, in the Glamorgan Record Office.

RUDC   Minutes of the Rhondda Urban District Council and committees, in the Glamorgan Record Office.

UDC   Urban District Council.

USA   Urban Sanitary Authority.

Acknowledgements

This study of the Rhondda's housing history would not have been possible without the assistance of many people. They should not, however, be implicated by any of my arguments, appraisals or conclusions.

Particular thanks are extended to Christopher Powell (Welsh School of Architecture), Hamish Richards (Cardiff), Lucy Dewhurst (Middlesex), W. John Smith (Manchester), Selwyn Baber, Morley and Clarence Fox (Ferndale) and Hugh James (Stephenson & Alexander, Cardiff).

Others who have assisted include Philip Jones (University of Hull), Geoff Wynn (University of the West of England, Bristol), Richard and Phyllis Price (Cwmparc), John Hingot (Trebanog), John Andrews (Llantwit Fardre), Diane Neal (Blaenllechau), and staff of Rhondda Housing Association, the Glamorgan Record, Office, Treorchy Library and the Ordnance Survey.

Thanks are extended to those who so spontaneously permitted surveys to be done inside their homes: Mr and Mrs H. Edwards (Ystrad), Mrs Bronwen Thompson (Wattstown), Mrs Amelia Thomas (Ystrad), Mrs Betty Williams (Ton Pentre), Mrs Jean Evans (Wattstown), Mrs Dora Wilding (Porth), Eddie Williams (Gelli), Mrs Edna Richardson (Llwynypia), Mr and Mrs J. Mortimer (Llwyncelyn), Mr and Mrs R. Locke (Ferndale), Mr and Mrs I. Phillips (Blaenycwm), Mr and Mrs B. Griffiths (Llwynypia), Mr and Mrs H. Williams (Ferndale), Mr D. Hardwick (Llwynypia), and Mrs Carol Collins (Penygraig).

While many of the photographs published here are my own, thanks are due to the following for permission to publish others: Christopher Powell (Plates 3, 4 and 7), Cyril Batstone (Front cover and Plate 9), *Western Mail and Echo* (Plate 6), Mrs Naomi Williams (Plate 2) and Mr T. Richards (Plate 10). The house plans were expertly drawn by Lydia Roberts, a student at the Welsh School of Architecture.

Finally, thanks are due to my family for their forbearance during the undertaking of this study.

University of Wales, Cardiff Malcolm J. Fisk
December 1995

1

Introduction

The history of housing in the Rhondda is closely linked to the development of the whole of the South Wales coalfield, itself an example of the most extreme kind of transformation that has befallen any community in Britain, one which shook these tranquil valleys out of centuries of rural solitude into a fervour of industrial activity and then to decay and decline.

The Rhondda comprises two valleys, the larger Rhondda Fawr (some nine and a half miles long) and the smaller Rhondda Fach (six and a half miles), whose rivers flow south-eastward to a confluence at Porth, before continuing to the Taff and thence to the Bristol Channel at Cardiff. The present borough has an area of some 24,000 acres, much of it barren mountain land over 1000ft above sea level. Modern boundaries closely reflect the catchment areas of the two rivers, although this was not the case in earlier times. The old parish of Ystradyfodwg parish included Rhigos (to the north of present-day Rhondda) and excluded the area from Williamstown through Dinas to Trebanog (which was in Llantrisant parish) and the area to the east of the river Rhondda Fach (which was in Llanwonno). Broadly speaking, these anomalies were overcome with the establishment of the Ystradyfodwg Urban Sanitary Authority in 1877, the forerunner of the Ystradyfodwg Urban District Council (formed in 1895), which became, by change of name in 1897, the Rhondda UDC.

This study examines the changes in Rhondda's housing from about 1800, when large-scale coalmining was still decades away, to the very different Rhondda of 1940. While the emphasis is on the agencies of housing provision and the evolution of different types of housing, note is taken of broader social, economic and political factors. These become particularly important in the second half of the period and combined to determine the characteristic types of housing that remain Rhondda's hallmark today.

This work joins other studies which have focused on this remarkable community, the most important of which was that by E.D. Lewis, originally published in 1958.[1] The story of the Rhondda is, in many respects, unique, since the speed of growth and decline are probably unequalled. The

---

[1] E.D. Lewis, *The Rhondda Valleys* (2nd ed., Cardiff, 1984).

population of the parish of Ystradyfodwg had stood at below 500 for centuries before the first census of 1801. By 1851 it had doubled to 951 and then trebled in each of the next three decades. By 1891 the population had reached over 50,000 and continued to rise rapidly to a peak of 167,000 in 1923–4. While the population grew, so did the extent of built-up areas. Building development was, however, rather more erratic on account of changes in housing demand, the success of new pits and other factors. The pace of development was generally so fast that the demand for housing only slackened for short periods in specific locations.

The speed of population growth sets the Rhondda apart from other Valley communities (and other coalfields) and means that it cannot be said to be characteristic of South Wales as a whole. Development started later than in the ironmaking towns, such as Aberdare, Merthyr Tydfil and Blaenavon, and because of the introduction of byelaws the Rhondda avoided some of the problems of haphazard, uncontrolled developments found in those places. The regularity of the streets in the Rhondda is clear from several of the photographs published here, including that on the front cover. Despite such layouts, however, the Rhondda was not spared the consequences of appalling sanitary conditions, overcrowding and ill-health.

The development of housing in the Rhondda must be seen within a broader context of Britain's Industrial Revolution and must take account not just of demand arising from the development of new industries but also of growing tensions between workers and employers, the growth of the labour movement and the development of local government institutions.

The period up to 1890 was relatively tranquil, a few men with money bringing the investment necessary to develop new industries or, in the case of Rhondda, to mine coal. Such men also dominated local administration. D. Byrne has labelled this period one of 'bourgeois democracy' in which local industries and local authorities were dominated by the capitalist classes.[1] From 1890 the situation began to change as public health, in particular, came to the fore. The local authorities, however, resisted taking on new obligations to improve public health since it was they (coming from the capitalist classes) who would be the first to pay for any increase in rates. In addition, they considered that sanitary reforms might jeopardise their position by giving working people some of the privileges which they enjoyed.[2]

---

[1] D. Byrne, 'Class and the local state', *International Journal of Urban and Regional Research*, 6 (1982), 65–7.

[2] D.S. Byrne et al., *Housing and health: the relationship between housing conditions and the health of council tenants* (Aldershot, 1986), pp. 11–12.

An event that initially helped focus attention (including, importantly, that of the capitalist classes) on public health was the publication in 1842 of Edwin Chadwick's *Report on the Sanitary Condition of the Labouring Population of Great Britain*.[1] Although imprecise in its recommendations, this clearly pointed out the cost to the nation of ill-health and high mortality (resulting in large numbers of widows and orphans) and the social cost of squalor and bad housing, in terms of poor morals, drunken behaviour etc. Though Chadwick ignored Wales (despite the appalling conditions at that time in the ironmaking towns) a Welsh dimension to the public health issue was given through the notorious Education Blue Books of 1847, which, while principally concerned with the quality of schooling, gave graphic accounts of often terrible housing conditions in both urban and rural communities, and noted the consequences for health and morality. Of Merthyr Tydfil it reported that:

> the state of Merthyr is disgraceful to those who are responsible for it. The vast majority of houses have no privies; where there is such a thing, it is a mere hole in the ground, with no drainage. Indeed, the town is in a very small degree drained at all. This is the case nearly all over Wales ... in a dense population, the consequences of such neglect are more loathsomely and degradingly apparent.[2]

While little improvement was to take place for more than three decades, the increasing importance of public health led to the formation of local sanitary authorities. The reluctance of such bodies to take effective action was, however, a key factor in bringing about further legislation to force the hands of the capitalists. Despite some improvements in health regulations, the incidence of ill-health, disease and death was still unacceptably high at the end of the century. The failure to deal effectively with housing problems within the broader framework of public health meant that a greater emphasis was being placed on housing as an issue in itself. There was, however, a threat to the capitalist classes. Housing, and access to it, had for centuries enabled divisions between the classes to be maintained and a perpetuation of the privileged position of the capitalists. The self-interest of the capitalist

---

[1] M.W. Flinn (ed.), *Report on the sanitary condition of the labouring population of Great Britain by Edwin Chadwick, 1842* (Edinburgh, 1965).

[2] *Reports of the Commissioners of Inquiry into the State of Education in Wales* (Parl. Papers, 1847, XXVII), p. 116.

classes would only be overcome through the growth of the labour movement and the pressure it would bring to secure major concessions.[1]

The pressure exercised by the labour movement became particularly strong at the end of the First World War and, as a consequence, the control of local administration by capitalist interests was finally broken.[2] The strength of working-class power led to an exceptional period during which the need for public housing was acknowledged nationally and, for two years, was supported by a generous government subsidy. This, however, was a short-term response to a temporary instability and as soon as greater 'control' could be exercised (and the labour movement again suppressed) the government were able to reduce the subsidies and reassert central control.[3] A commitment to some form of public housing, however, had been established and, despite the imposition of greater controls on council house building, it was accepted as one mechanism to overcome some of the problems presented by the slums. Ironically much of the new public housing that was developed had rent levels that were outside the reach of the poorest families. This was a result of the Ministry of Health's insistence on rents which would, on the one hand, help councils repay their loans but, on the other, meant that the houses were not rented to people in the greatest housing need. The 'generous' subsidy that derived from the 1919 legislation might, in such a context, be regarded as inadequate.

The capitalist classes, while losing much of their power within local government, were able to retain their strength in other areas, notably employment. In the Rhondda the colliery owners tried to maintain profitability in the face of foreign competition, difficult working conditions and increasing conflicts with the workers. The Rhondda's decline was now under way. The community lost a third of its population between 1921 and 1951, a decline described as 'probably the highest in Europe'.[4] Such extreme changes suggest that the key to Rhondda's housing history lies not in a national context but in its unique local circumstances. The types and tenures of housing and the agencies of provision reflect this uniqueness and help an understanding of some aspects of the evolution of housing in industrial communities.

---

[1] See, e.g., P. Malpass and A. Murie, *Housing policy and practice* (1987), pp. 32–3, 45.

[2] J. Melling (ed.), *Housing, social policy and the state* (Beckenham, 1980), p. 31.

[3] J. Dale, 'Class struggle, social policy and state structure: central-local relations and housing policy, 1919–39', in Melling (ed.), *Housing*, p. 220.

[4] D. Egan, *Coal society: a history of the South Wales mining valleys, 1840–1980* (Llandysul, 1987), p. 126.

2

The Pre-Industrial Period

It is but a tiny span of time since the exploitation of coal so rudely transformed Rhondda's two valleys. Indeed, centuries had passed in which human settlement was sparse and evidence of any activity was absent for mile upon mile of mixed woodland and barren hillsides. Less than two hundred years ago there were no towns or villages. B.H. Malkin, in his journey through the Rhondda in 1803, noted the absence of settlements all the way from Newbridge (Pontypridd) to Pont Neath Vechan, although there were occasional clusters of labourers' cottages, as at Penyrenglyn, Ystrad and Pontygwaith. As well as noting the beauty of the 'rich and verdant' meadows next to the 'wild and romantic' mountains, Malkin also saw the poverty of the local hill farmers who lived in the humblest of dwellings.[1]

Cottages

The simplicity of the dwellings reflected the fact that the farm labourer would build his home according to his and his family's needs and resources. Many such dwellings were *'tai un nos'* ('one-night houses'), built overnight in makeshift fashion using whatever materials were to hand. The floor would be mud, the walls mud and stone (with tiny unglazed windows), and the roof normally thatched with rushes or ferns. It was believed that if *tai un nos* could be built overnight and a fire was burning in the hearth by the morning, the builder would become the owner of the house and the surrounding land as far as an axe could be thrown.[2] Such cottages were, needless to say, often so flimsy as to last just a few months, by which time the labourer, having established his 'claim', would rebuild or replace his dwelling with a more permanent (though still humble) structure.

---

[1] B.H. Malkin, *The scenery, antiquities and biography of South Wales* (Repr. Wakefield, 1970).
[2] M.I. Williams, 'A general view of Glamorgan houses and their interiors in the seventeenth and eighteenth centuries', *Glamorgan Historian*, 10 (1974), 159–62; E. Wiliam, *Home-made homes: dwellings of the rural poor in Wales* (Cardiff, 1988), p. 13.

Many dwellings, and the living conditions of the inhabitants, would have been as miserable as those described in the House of Commons in 1844, when Richard Cobden said of the Welsh farm labourers that they

> live in mud huts, with only one room for sleeping, cooking and eating—different ages and sexes herding together. Their cottages have no windows but a hole in the mud wall to admit air and light, into which a bundle of rags or turf is thrust at night to stop it up. The thinly thatched roofs are seldom drop-dry and the mud floor becomes consequently damp and wet, and dirty almost as the road; and to complete the wretched picture, huddled in the corner are the rags and straw of which their beds are composed.[1]

The poverty of farms in the Rhondda is illustrated by the survival on the Bute estate in the early nineteenth century of flails and wooden ploughs. Walter Davies noted in 1813 that 'The stock carried by many Bute farms was inadequate in quantity and quality'. The total stock of the 654 acre farm of Ystradfechan in 1831 consisted of six 'poor little cows', four calves, one heifer, three old mares and 'about fifty poor sheep'.[2]

Upland Glamorgan contrasted dramatically with the better conditions in the Vale to the south, where cottages tended to be stone built (as opposed to mud and stone) and have roofs thatched with better materials or covered by stone tiles. The creation of rooms (enabling at least some separation of sleeping and living areas) was achieved by using light partitions or by the arrangement of whatever modest furniture the household possessed. In the late eighteenth century such a cottage would be likely to measure some 24ft by 14ft overall and would have cost about £20 to build.[3]

In the Rhondda, design took second place to utility. Where more permanent structures were built instead of, or to replace, *tai un nos*, these would, at least in part, have used available local stone. The designs remained simple, offering little more than space than that provided by cottages built of mud and turf. One such cottage in Rhondda has survived, Tŷ Du, Cymmer (Fig. 2.1). The single-roomed cottage, with rubble walls some 2ft

---

[1] Quoted in E. Gauldie, *Cruel habitations: a history of working-class housing 1780–1918* (1974), p. 13.

[2] J. Davies, 'Glamorgan and the Bute Estate, 1766–1947' (University of Wales [Aberystwyth] Ph.D. thesis, 1969), p. 406.

[3] Williams, 'Glamorgan houses', p. 163.

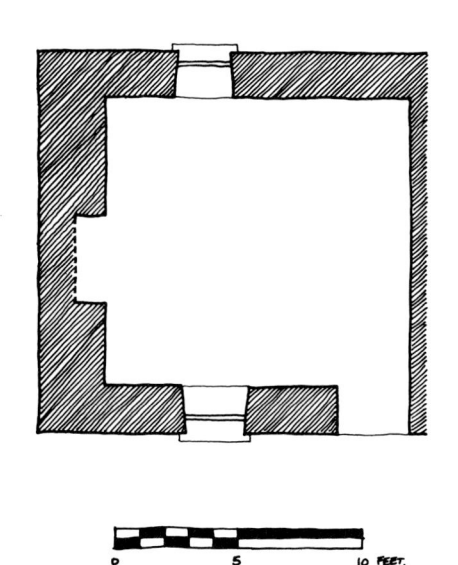

2.1 Tŷ Du, Cymmer

6in. thick, was originally thatched. A loft would have been reached by a ladder to give some additional, though limited, sleeping accommodation.[1]

The better cottages in Rhondda were, in most cases, rented from local freeholders or, like the farms themselves, leased from one or other of the great estates. The concern of the estates for the upkeep of their land and buildings ensured that some consideration, at least, began to be given to cottage design. Farms inherited by the second Marquess of Bute, for instance, were described as in a 'deplorable condition', which led him to spend a substantial proportion of the estate income on improvements.[2]

Cottages increasingly came to resemble larger dwellings, though on a smaller scale. The dominant form in Wales, including probably the Rhondda, was the 'end-chimney central doorway' type. This has a fireplace at the gable end (heating the living room), and a parlour at the other end (Fig. 2.2).[3] Needless to say, because the cottages were small, overcrowding was widespread, although this was in some part overcome during the nineteenth century by incorporating lofts or half lofts, reached by ladders (as at Tŷ Du) or, later again, by stone staircases.[4]

Farmhouses

The best standard of building was to be found among the farmhouses which, together with their byres, provided shelter, not only for the farmer and his family, but also for farm workers (who, when they married, would be asked to move out to a cottage). On the whole, the farms were of the type traditionally found throughout Glamorgan, with at least three or four rooms and an upper storey. Many were in the form of the Welsh long house (*tŷ hir*) and were generally held on either long leases or yearly tenancies. In 1892 just 1 per cent of Glamorgan farmers were freeholders.[5]

Only one long house in Rhondda survives in roughly its original form, Tyntyla Farm, Ystrad (Fig. 2.3; Plate 1). Others have been lost, or are in ruins (e.g. Dinas Isaf, Penygraig) or have been substantially altered (e.g.

---

[1] I am indebted to Christopher Powell of the Welsh School of Architecture for permission to redraw his plans of Tŷ Du.

[2] Davies, Thesis, p. 32.

[3] P. Smith, *Houses of the Welsh countryside: a study in historical geography* (1975), pp. 313–14.

[4] I. Peate, *The Welsh house* (Liverpool, 1946), pp. 93ff.

[5] J. Davies, 'The end of the great estates and the rise of freehold farming in Wales', *Welsh History Review*, 7 (1974), 187.

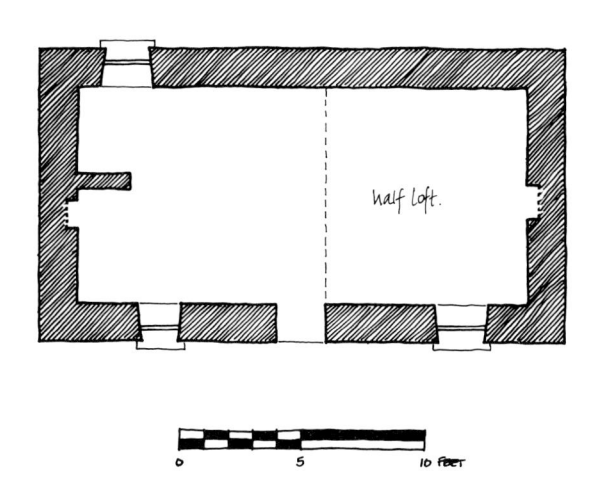

2.2 Typical cottage farm

Nant Dyris Ycha, Blaenllechau.[1] The long house is the characteristic type of farmhouse in south-east Wales, where the farmer, his family, some of his labourers and his animals would live under one roof. A definition is offered by S.R. Jones and J.T. Smith as including 'all buildings which shelter both a family and their cattle, and have direct access between the two parts'. Its origins possibly date back to the fourteenth and fifteenth centuries, though the inclusion of an upper storey is an innovation of the two centuries that followed.[2] Of the Vaynor and Penderyn district (adjoining Ystradyfodwg to the north) Smith and Jones noted that 'long houses so predominate over all other types of houses that they must be given pride of place'.[3] The same is true of the Rhondda, where there are few other farmhouse types that date back to the seventeenth and eighteenth centuries.

The design of long houses is characterised by Tyntyla Farm, which is set in an excavated hollow at right angles to the mountainside. The byre is at a lower level to the house and is reached directly by a door from the living accommodation. The ground floor comprises a living room and a dairy. It is linked to the upper floor bedrooms by a curved stone stairway alongside a massive fireplace. The slightly narrower width of the byre suggests that the building was built in two stages. The walls are nearly 3ft thick, supporting a roof structure with massive trusses. This is now covered by imported slates but was originally covered by locally quarried stone tiles. The ground floor is covered by stone flags. The main entrance to the hayloft from the farmyard remains via a ladder. A subsidiary means of access from a first floor room leads to a steep flight of stone stairs to an upper loft where unmarried farm labourers would have slept.

In other farms the byre was not connected directly to the living quarters. Such farmhouses sometimes shared with Tyntyla central and gable fireplaces and had entrances to the side of the central chimney (e.g. Troedyrhiw Farm, Porth). In other long houses there was direct entry at the centre of the house and no central chimney (e.g. Bodringallt and Hafod Fach, Porth).

In 1847 there were about 70 farms in the Rhondda, together with a number of smallholdings. They were spread unevenly with some concentration in the upper Rhondda Fawr. The remoteness of the area meant that each farm practised essentially 'subsistence' agriculture, the mainstay of which

---

[1] P.R. Davies, *Historic Rhondda: an archaeological and topographical survey, 800 BC – AD 1850* (Treorchy, 1989), pp. 37–58.

[2] S.R. Jones and J.T. Smith, 'The houses of Breconshire. Part 1: The Builth district', *Brycheiniog*, 9 (1963), p. 5; I. Peate, 'The long house again', *Folk Life*, 2 (1964), pp. 57–8.

[3] S.R. Jones and J.T. Smith, 'The houses of Breconshire. Part 6: The Faenor and Penderyn district', *Brycheiniog*, 16 (1988), p. 4.

THE PRE-INDUSTRIAL PERIOD 17

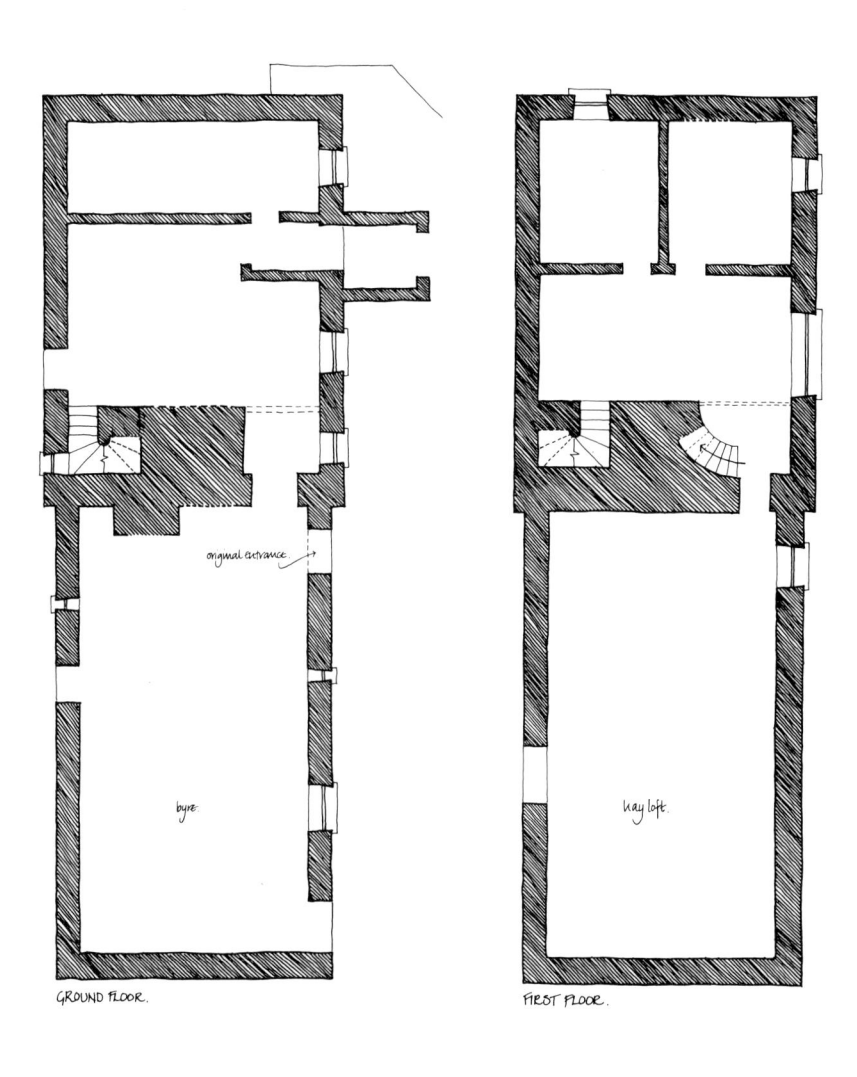

GROUND FLOOR.

original entrance

byre

FIRST FLOOR.

hay loft

0 5 feet

2.3 Tyntyla Farm, Ystrad

was sheep, supplemented by cattle, pigs and a limited quantity of crops. This hard and simple way of life was to change abruptly with the exploitation of the wealth of coal under the soil, as the Rhondda was thrust into its first phase of industrial development. The simple styles of building were to change as industrialisation brought a massive demand for new housing and also for migrants with building skills. The farms and cottages were, however, to retain a parallel role for another 30 years in parts of the Rhondda, by which time most, if not all, the poorer cottages had been abandoned.

3

Housing during the Early Period of Industrial Development 1840–79

The first attempts to exploit coal in the Rhondda on any scale were made by Walter Coffin, whose activities around Dinas can now be seen as heralding the rapid development that was to take place during the second half of the nineteenth century. While he was the first to sink a shaft to reach the rich seams of Rhondda coal in 1812, it was not until the 1840s that others followed in his footsteps and sank shafts elsewhere. Among the new entrepreneurs were D.W. James at Porth, Leonard Hadley at Troedyrhiw and Messrs Shepherd and Evans at Ynyshir. From this time onwards the development of collieries and new communities gathered pace.[1] Others, while not directly involved in the sinking of pits and the mining of coal, bought farms in the Rhondda. The Bute estate, for instance, was extended and Crawshay Bailey, originally an ironmaster, began to purchase a number of farms. The estates were thus able to lease land for colliery development, housing or commercial use and enjoyed a steady and increasing income as more building took place.

During the early period of coal mining, there was little housing in the Rhondda and many colliery owners found it necessary to build houses for their workers. By 1841 Walter Coffin owned 46 houses in Dinas, most of which commanded a gross annual rental of between £2 and £2 10s. His colliery was by this time the largest producer of sea-sale coal in Glamorgan, employing 301 men and 112 boys.[2] His properties, however, were exceptionally small and had more in common with the cottages of farm labourers than the houses which were to follow during the main period of industrialisation. Largely due to Coffin, Rhondda's population rose to 1,140 by 1841, of whom 70 per cent were under 30. There was a clear predomi-

---

[1] Lewis, *Rhondda Valleys*, p. 52.
[2] Ibid., p. 44.

nance of men, a reflection of the significance of immigration in this early period.[1]

While some colliery owners built houses, the estate owners did not. The single known exception was the Bute estate, which built some 50 to 60 houses around 1850 at Treherbert following the successful sinking of a shaft at Cwmsaerbren by the Bute Merthyr Colliery.[2]

The most common form of house comprised four rooms on two floors, i.e. a living room, scullery and two upstairs bedrooms reached by a tightly curved stone staircase. Such houses often had second entrances at the rear and hence were known as *'tai bac a ffrynt'*. Rents were 2s or 3s a week. The houses were invariably built of locally quarried Pennant sandstone and roofed with stone tiles or (increasingly) imported slate. For instance, small houses built by the colliery proprietor George Insole at Cymmer and America Fach, Porth, were roofed with slates from Bangor in North Wales.[3]

The extent of early development was small. The first immigrants founded the villages of Store House, Graig Ddu, Dinas, Eirw and Cymmer, whilst almost all of the remainder of the Rhondda retained its rural tranquillity.[4] C.G. Powell noted an informal and haphazard layout of dwellings at this time, most blocks of which he classifies as 'small'. Some 71 dwellings, however, were in what he termed 'mass' houses, which were terraced and likely to be newer housing accompanying the colliery development. A terrace at Gyfeillon (Trehafod) may have been the only local example of back-to-back houses.[5]

Many houses of this period offered little more space than the rural cottages that preceded them (and still abounded in the area). Examples are provided by the six cottages grouped around Cymmer Chapel (all but one of which still survive). One terrace of three included two one-up one-down cottages (27 High Street and 20 School Street) and a larger cottage (28 High Street; Fig. 3.1).[6] A similar 'square plan' terrace of one-up one-down cottages is Penygefnen, Dinas. One of the cottages here has a floor area of just 205 sq.ft. (Fig. 3.2). Another example is Tŷ Mellyn, Dinas.

The lower Rhondda was clearly being transformed and, although the houses, like the farm labourers' cottages, represented simple styles, they

---

[1] C.G. Powell, 'Occupation and form of early Rhondda housing' (Unpublished).
[2] Davies, Thesis, p. 437.
[3] Lewis, *Rhondda Valleys*, pp. 182–3.
[4] Ibid., p. 15.
[5] Powell, 'Occupation and form'.
[6] I am indebted to Mr Powell for permission to redraw his plans of 28 High Street and Penygefnen.

EARLY INDUSTRIAL HOUSING 21

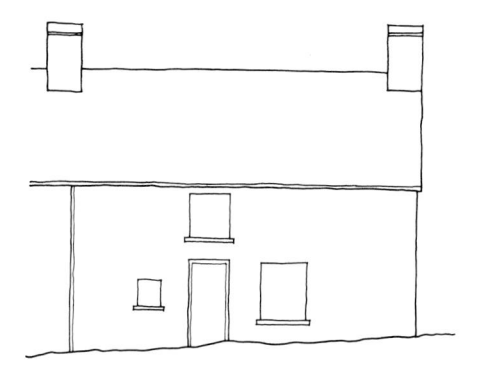

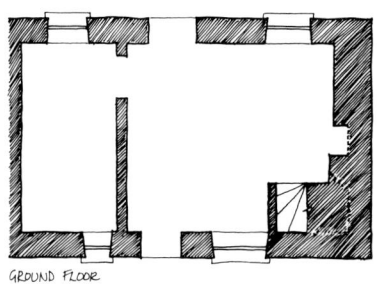

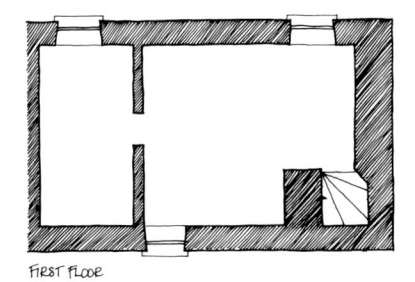

GROUND FLOOR

FIRST FLOOR

0 5 10 FEET

3.1 28 High Street, Cymmer

3.2 Penygefnen, Dinas

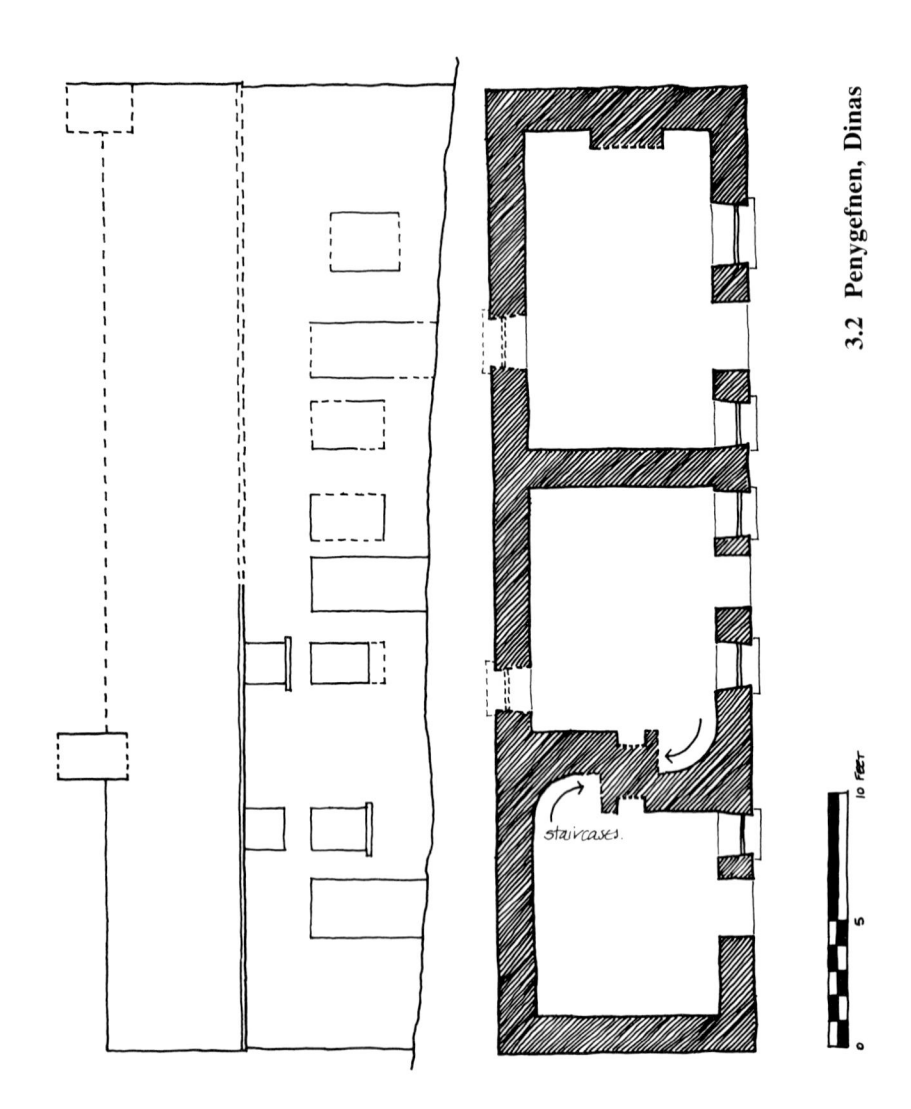

were increasingly occupied by families who gained their livelihood from the pits (notably those of Walter Coffin). Powell notes three main house types at this time: square form one-up one-down (including Penygefnen, Dinas); narrow frontage, four rooms with no rear entry; and wide frontage, four rooms and blind or near blind backs (i.e. often without windows at the rear, such as 28 High Street, Cymmer). The smaller types would, in the next decade or so, cease to be built as there was a move from 'small' housing to 'mass' housing in the areas of colliery development.[1]

The fate of farms

In what remained of 'rural' Rhondda more farmland was bring bought up, notably by Crawshay Bailey who, with his brother Joseph, was an ironmaster at Blaina and Nantyglo. With a clear eye for commercial potential he bought fifteen Rhondda farms, and other land elsewhere (Pontypridd, Mountain Ash and Cwm, Ebbw Vale). Crawshay Bailey was described as an 'old fashioned eccentric, farmer looking', of whom it was said that 'the finest stroke of business of his life was in purchasing a group of farms in the Rhondda Valley', which produced an income in 1888 of £30,000 a year.[2] The Bute estate at this time included Abergorki, Ystradfechan, Llethr Ddu, Tynewydd and Tonllwyd farms in the Rhondda. Another major local landowner was the Earl of Dunraven.

There was no turning back. Further investment led to the establishment of a number of new communities in the Rhondda. At the same time, road, rail and tramway links to Pontypridd and the coast were progressively improved. More and more woodland areas, grasslands and farms were destroyed by the collieries, their spoil and the houses, shops, chapels, pubs, lodging houses and hotels that were needed to serve a rapidly growing population. Most of the farms in the Rhondda were to lose all their better quality grazing land to the new urban sprawl.

A good example of the extent and speed of change is provided by the Bute farms at Tynewydd and Tonllwyd (Treherbert). Here the estate's income from farm rents declined (through the loss of farmland) from £90 a year in 1859 to just £6 in 1875. The compensating income from leases on land for housing or other development and the sale of timber from trees cut

---

[1] Powell, 'Occupation and form'.

[2] B.D. Jones, *Early history of the Rhondda Valley. Baptist Centenary 1810–1910* (Pontypridd, 1910), p. 8.

down was substantial, enabling farming to be subsidised and farm rents to be kept down.[1]

For those farms that remained, the emphasis on subsistence diminished as better communications opened up new markets for their products. For some (e.g. on the Bute estate) there was the additional benefit of modernisation.[2] The humbler tenants' cottages, however, were abandoned as labourers were able to rent more soundly built houses in the new villages.

The emergence of industrial housing

The pace of colliery development and of immigration was not matched by adequate housing provision. Overcrowding was commonplace and, in Dinas, tenants in Coffin's properties were forced to take in a minimum of two lodgers.[3] Colliery owners, on the whole, continued to provide accommodation for their workers, often initially by the erection of wooden huts to be replaced later by stone built houses. 'Encampments' of wooden huts at this time included those at Fernhill and Dunraven Collieries, Blaenrhondda, and the 22 wooden dwellings at Baptist Square and Mountain Row, Blaenllechau.[4]

The houses built up to 1860 were generally smaller than those which followed and included a variety of styles. Most were built on relatively flat or gently sloping sites, so that the additional work (and costs) of building retaining walls, cutting and filling etc was kept to a minimum. On the other hand, houses at Long Row, Blaenllechau (Plate 2), a community settled over the mountain from Aberdare rather than from lower Rhondda, were built on the steeper, southern facing slopes in preference to easier slopes on the other side of the valley. Most therefore have substantial retaining walls and may be some of the Rhondda's earliest examples of two-storey properties with an additional lower storey giving access to a garden at the rear.[5]

---

[1] Davies, Thesis, p. ix.

[2] Ibid., p. 410.

[3] H. Williams, *Davies the Ocean: railway king and coal tycoon* (Cardiff, 1991), p. 89.

[4] P.N. Jones, 'Aspects of the population and settlement geography of the South Wales coalfield, 1850–1926' (Birmingham University Ph.D. thesis, 1965), p. 252; N. Williams, *A history of Blaenllechau School* (Ferndale, 1979), chapter 3.

[5] A survey of 'Labour and the poor in metropolitan, rural and manufacturing districts of England and Wales', conducted by the *Morning Chronicle* in 1849–51, noted three-storey workmen's cottages in Aberdare and Sirhowy: J. Ginswick (ed.), *Labour and the poor in England and Wales, 1849–51. 3. South Wales and North Wales* (London, 1983), p. 134.

An example of property developed in this period is 32 Mary Street, Porth (Fig. 3.3). This is one of a pair of small cottages with an entrance passage at the centre of the dwelling off which are two small rooms, one of which is the pantry with just one small window.[1] The other front room is a small scullery. The passage leads through to a living room with a spiral stone stair giving access to two bedrooms. There is no landing, one bedroom being reached through the other. Another example is 8 Railway Terrace, Cwmparc (Fig. 3.4). This is a single-fronted property where the front door opens, via a small vestibule, to the living room. Off this is a further room and a passage to the rear scullery. The tightly curved spiral stair is squeezed into the corner of the living room, between the fireplace and the front wall. It rises to two bedrooms with (as at Mary Street, Porth) 'through' access.

The two-storey single-fronted house was the most common type in the Rhondda at this period. Isolated terraces of single-storey cottages were, however, built, one of which is Glanselsig Terrace, Blaenycwm (Fig. 3.5; Plate 3), where four rooms with fireplaces surround a central chimney.[2] The most notable characteristic of such early dwellings is the variety of individual features. This began to disappear after 1860 when a consensus emerged about the most 'efficient' designs. Less efficient house layouts were not used and we enter a period where it is easier to distinguish between house types (notably between single- and double-fronted forms).

An example of this period after 1860 is 19 Ton Row, Ton Pentre (Fig. 3.6). The lower part of Ton Row was built in 1865 on Crawshay Bailey land by the colliery proprietor David Davies of Llandinam and his partners Abraham Howell of Welshpool, Morgan Joseph of Ystradfechan, John Osborne Riches of Aberdare, Esra Roberts of Tenby and Thomas Webb, also of Llandinam.[3] The same partnership had sunk the adjoining Ocean Colliery the previous year. It is said that when David Davies sought a lease to mine coal, Crawshay Bailey replied that he 'did not like to part with his land to adventurers'. Davies is said to have retorted, 'I am no adventurer, but an honest trader, and for every honest guinea you will put down, I will put another'. A deal was then struck between them.[4] The lease by Crawshay Bailey estate for the housing development was typical of others that were to

---

[1] 32 St Mary Street, although it has a central doorway, has dimensions similar to single-fronted properties. The tiny size of the front room also gives it more in common with single-fronted dwellings than other house forms.

[2] While the design of properties at Glanselsig, Blaenycwm, is rare in the Rhondda, similar dwellings (without the central chimney) are found elsewhere in the Valleys (e.g. at Cymmer Afan and Ystradgynlais).

[3] Lease in private hands.

[4] Johns, *Early history*, p. 8.

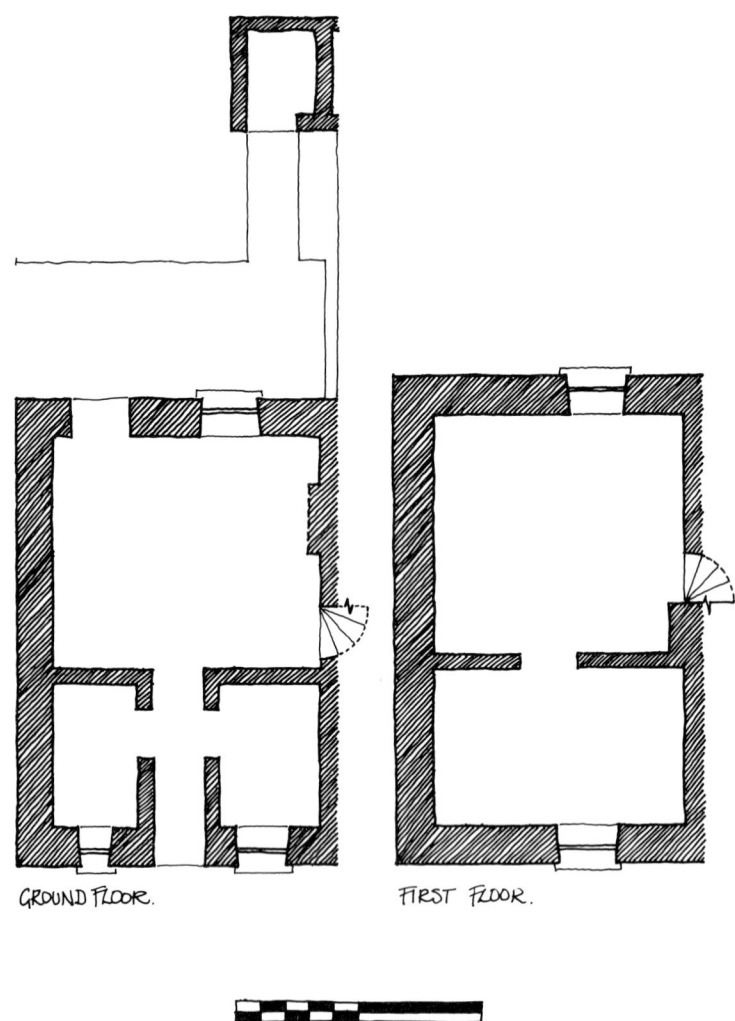

GROUND FLOOR.   FIRST FLOOR.

0 5 10 FEET.

3.3 32 Mary Street, Porth

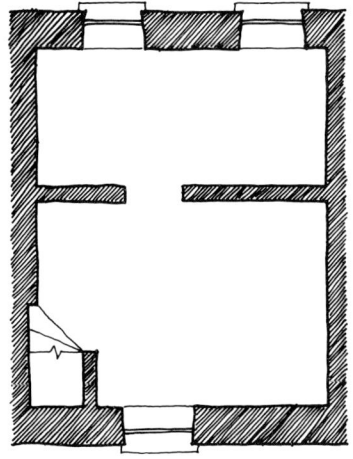

FIRST FLOOR.

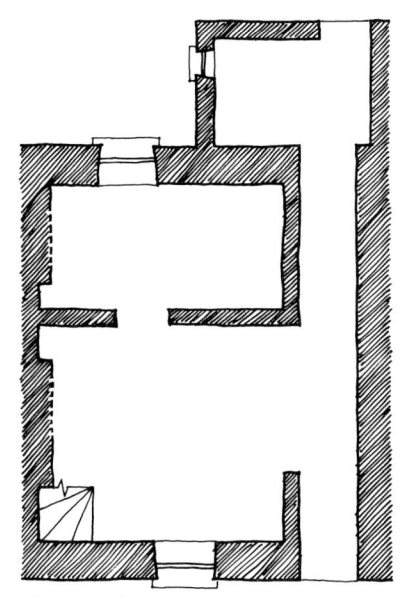

GROUND FLOOR.

3.4 8 Railway Terrace, Cwmparc

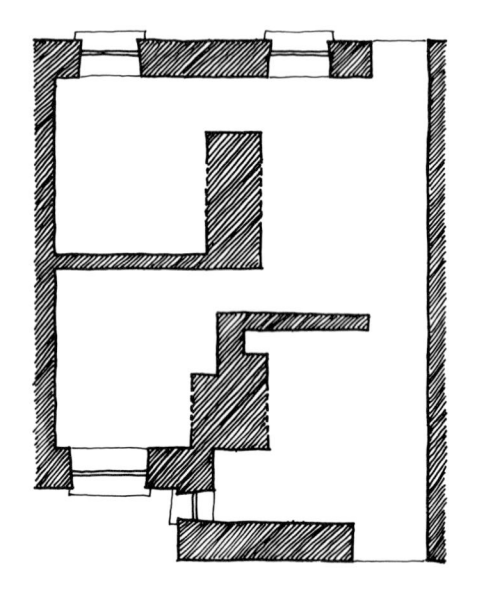

3.5   4 Glanselsig Terrace, Blaenycwm

FIRST FLOOR.

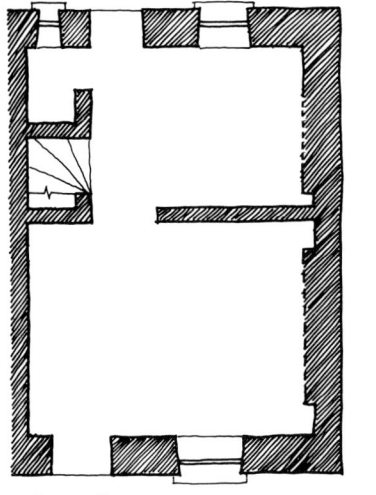

GROUND FLOOR.

3.6 19 Ton Row, Ton Pentre

follow. It was for 99 years and related to 19 dwellings on a plot of 1r 35p. Whilst giving various 'easements, privileges and rights', the lease excluded all mineral rights underlying the properties. The usual clauses requiring the leaseholder to repair and maintain the property and not to carry out the trades of 'Tavernkeeper, Alehouse Keeper, Retailer of Beer or any Spirituous Liquors ... or any noisome, dangerous or offensive trades' were also included. The ground rent was £8 11s 6d per year.

This venture was successful and the Ocean Colliery Co. (i.e. David Davies and his partners) went on to develop similar small houses in the upper part of Ton Row, in Parry Street and elsewhere, eventually owning several hundred in total.[1] The houses in Ton Row are single-fronted with two downstairs rooms (with fireplaces) and a pantry, but are generous in providing three (admittedly small) upstairs bedrooms. Interestingly (and unusually for this period) the curved stair is of timber, not stone, and bricks are used in the chimney and flue.

The second, less common, property type of this period is the double-fronted house. These are narrow in depth (thereby reducing the roof timber spans) and often have entrances via both front and rear lanes. An example of the double-fronted house of this period is the 'Scotch' terraces at Llwynypia, built by Scotsman Archibald Hood, owner of the Glamorgan (Scotch) Colliery sunk in 1863. The terraces, built from 1865 onwards, total over 200 houses rising up the valley side and backing on to narrow access lanes. They all have long front gardens. 3 Holyrood Terrace is typical (Fig. 3.7), with two ground floor and three upstairs rooms. The closet is across the rear lane and up a flight of steps. There are five windows on the front (easterly elevation) of the house but only two at the rear. The ground floors are laid with flagstones, the use of brick being confined to chimneys and flues. Roofs are of imported Welsh slates.

As this period progressed so house styles developed. Room sizes increased, as did the number and size of windows. In addition, small rear scullery extensions began to appear on single-fronted properties.

The sanitary dimension

Changes in house design reflected increasing local anxiety about public health, as people became aware of the squalor of many of Britain's industrial towns, including nearby Aberdare and Merthyr Tydfil. The concern was clearly justified: towns were unpaved with open sewers and no arrangements

---

[1] Williams, *Davies the Ocean*, p. 96.

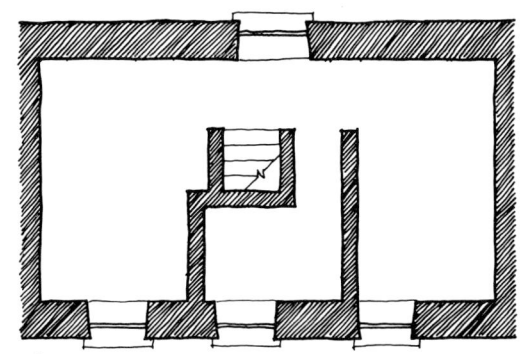

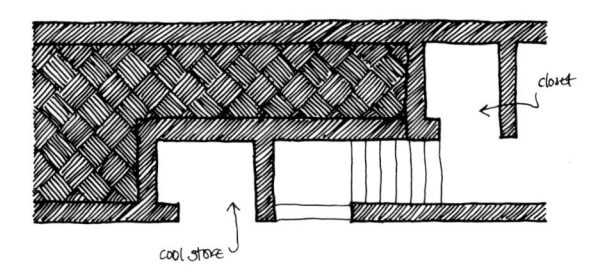

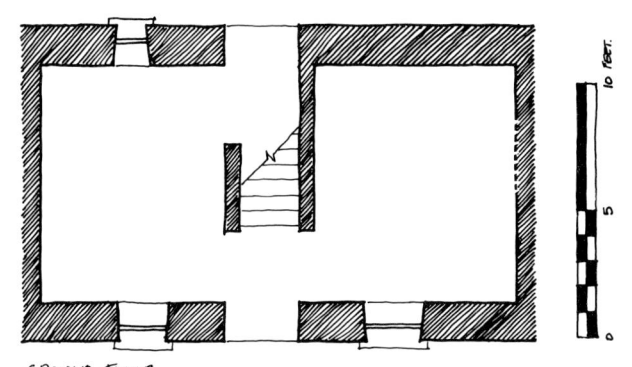

3.7 3 Holyrood Terrace, Llwynypia

for the removal of human waste, apart from sale to local farmers for manure. The rivers were both receptacles of waste and a major source of water. Chadwick's report, using evidence from England and Scotland, but not Wales, pointed to the direct relationship of insanitary conditions to disease and death; the economic costs of ill-health to families, with people often unavailable or unable to work; the effects on morality of bad housing, through different sexes having to share bedrooms; and the inefficiency of existing administrative procedures.[1]

The 1848 Public Health Act which followed was the first acknowledgement by the government that they had some responsibility for public health. The Act allowed for the setting up of local boards of health where the death rate was more than 23 per 1,000 a year or where a petition was submitted by one-tenth of the ratepayers. The boards had to appoint medical officers of health and had powers over street cleaning, paving, sewerage and water supplies. The legislation was a beginning, but most Welsh towns remained outside its scope. The national cholera epidemics of 1849, 1854 and 1867, however, helped increase awareness and, in the words of M.W. Flinn, 'stirred even the moribund, degraded, unreformed municipal corporations into fits of unwonted sanitary activity. It was the clearest warning of the lethal propensities of the swollen towns of the industrial area.'[2]

Such concerns influenced plans for development on land owned by the various estates in the Rhondda. The spacious layout of roads on the Bute estate in Treorchy and Treherbert, for instance, is testimony to at least some interest in planning and design, although the squares and public gardens found on the estate in Cardiff are absent.[3] Both the Bute and Crawshay Bailey estates employed inspectors to supervise and monitor the laying out of building land and housing developments. The creation of 'compact' communities was thereby brought about, together with the provision of sewers and other services.

Houses on the Bute estate included Dumfries Street, Treorchy, where in the 1870s ground rents of £1 10s were payable on properties with a frontage of 16ft. Colliery company housing on Bute estate land included 1-52 Glynrhondda Street and 166-8 Bute Street, Treorchy, leased to Burnyeat Brown & Co.[4]

---

[1] Flinn (ed.), *Sanitary condition*, p. 58.
[2] Ibid., p. 8.
[3] J. Davies, *Cardiff and the Marquesses of Bute* (Cardiff, 1981), pp. 204–5.
[4] Ibid., p. 208.

Model dwellings

A further influence at this time may have been the 'model' dwellings and villages built by some industrialists and philanthropists elsewhere in Britain. An interesting attempt to emulate such models was made at Tynewydd by Thomas Joseph who had opened colliery levels at Blaenycwm in the late 1850s and 1860s. It has been suggested that Joseph was influenced by the work of the Welshman Robert Owen at New Lanark in Scotland and of the industrialist Titus Salt at Saltaire, Yorkshire, but a more likely influence is that provided nearby by the model village at Abercarn, developed by the colliery proprietor Benjamin Hall, and Butetown (Rhymney), by the ironworks manager Richard Johnson.[1]

Joseph's proposed developed was to have taken place at Clyngwyn, Blaenrhondda, but, following lengthy correspondence with the landowner (the Dunraven estate), a site at Tynewydd was selected instead. The village, to be known as Brynwyndham, was to comprise 116 houses of three types to 'meet the wants of different classes of families' (Fig. 3.8). The third class houses, of which there were to be 20, had just two rooms and a tiny scullery—very humble indeed for 'model' dwellings—and it is small wonder that the Dunraven estate insisted that better standards be achieved. The second class dwellings, on the other hand, had two downstairs and two upstairs rooms. No record of the first class dwellings survives. The enterprise did not come to fruition and eventually just 20 somewhat inferior dwellings were built at Scott Street and Wyndham Street, Tynewydd, with a further 60 houses built later on the land by the London & South Wales Co. to whom Joseph sold his interests in 1872.[2]

The growing crisis in public health

The improvements in housing standards prior to 1872 made little impact on public health. In any case, it was argued in 1860 that the miner of the lower Rhondda was on the whole 'better housed than his counterpart in the older industrial areas of South Wales and since the district was still largely rural ... he was spared those fearful scourges of smallpox, cholera and diphtheria

---

[1] J.R. Davies, 'Brynwyndham village, upper Rhondda Fawr', *Morgannwg*, 20 (1976), 53–4; L.B. Collier, 'A detailed survey of the South Wales coal industry from *c.* 1750 to *c.* 1850' (London University Ph.D. thesis, 1940), p. 373; J. van Laun, 'Butetown, Rhymney: a conservation area?' (Unpublished paper given to Ironbridge Institute, 1984).

[2] Davies, 'Brynwyndham', pp. 55, 62.

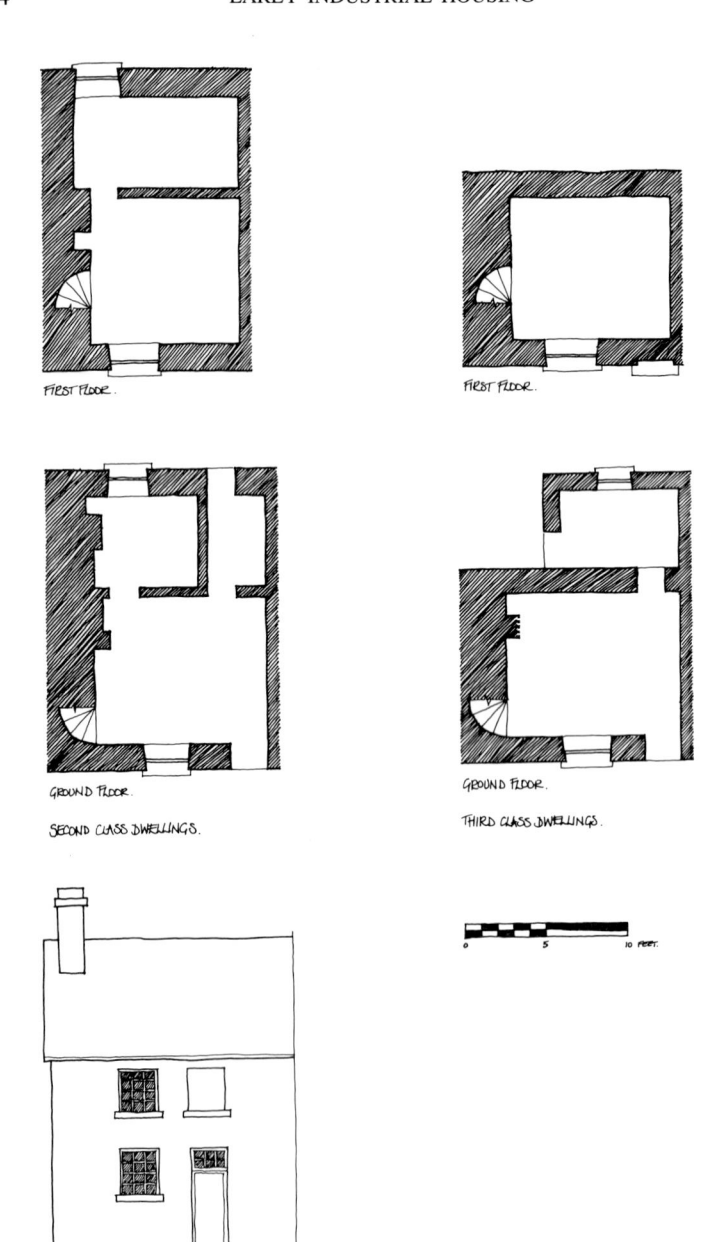

3.8 Houses planned for Brynwyndham Village, Treherbert

which from time to time ravaged human life in crowded towns like Merthyr Tydfil'.[1] The situation quickly changed for the worse. Just a decade later a report on sanitary conditions in the Rhondda in 1870 concluded that 'there is an extreme neglect of all sanitary precautions. There is no due provision for excrement and refuse disposal. Water supply is totally insufficient and liable to pollution'.[2] The same report drew attention to 34 deaths due to cholera and seven from diarrhoea in the parish of Ystradyfodwg during 1866. Partly as a result of this report Ystradyfodwg Sewer Authority was set up to deal with sanitary matters in the district.

While provision for waste and refuse disposal was sadly lacking, services supplying water and street lighting operated over a large part of Rhondda. The Ystrad Gas & Water Co., established in 1868, provided gas lighting for the streets of the middle Rhondda Fawr and water for most of that valley. The Ferndale Gas Co. provided street lighting for the Rhondda Fach whilst water in this smaller valley (and the lower Rhondda Fawr) was supplied by the Pontypridd Water Works Co., established in 1864. Various collieries in both valleys supplied water to several thousand houses.[3]

By the time the Ystradyfodwg Urban Sanitary Authority was established in 1877, the situation in Rhondda had become as bad as neighbouring Aberdare and Merthyr Tydfil. The newly appointed medical officer of health noted, in his report to one of the first meetings of the authority, the need for attention to three key areas, stating that

> People have been permitted to erect houses without any formation of streets and roads and without any system. The drainage has been rendered difficult in consequence and in many cases totally neglected as well as a proper supply of offices to each house ... I have noticed cottages in this District in which two or more families live in the same building; and those who inhabit underground apartments have their children invariably suffering from wasting diseases.[4]

Despite such circumstances the authority initially declined to exercise the powers conferred on it by the 1875 Public Health Act.[5] They did, however, quickly reverse this decision and appointed an inspector of nuisances in addition to the medical officer. They also took action against those

---

[1] Lewis, *Rhondda Valleys*, p. 183.
[2] Ibid., p. 203.
[3] Ibid., p. 205.
[4] Glamorgan Record Office, Ystradyfodwg USA, 25 Jan. 1878.
[5] Ibid., 17 Jan. 1878.

responsible for public health offences who were mostly the owners of privately rented properties. In 1878, for instance, notices were served on William Pope of the Gas Works, Dowlais, in respect of four cottages in Treorchy; on Thomas Davies of Gelli Farm, Ystrad, in respect of six cottages at Troedyrhiw, Porth; on Evan Cule, a grocer of Treherbert, in respect of three cottages at Penyrenglyn; and on David Jones, a miller of Graig Ddu, Dinas, in respect of five cottages at Red Cow Row, Treorchy. These were cases of privies in an 'abominable' state.[1]

Not every house, however, had its own privy, many having to share with neighbours. The medical officer reported, for instance, on outbreaks of enteric fever and typhoid at the Upper Bute Huts, Treherbert, noting that 'the huts are not drained and have no privy accommodation of any sort and their water supply is unsatisfactory in the extreme'. He ordered the building of 'proper and efficient' water closets within 21 days, although it appears that the huts were instead demolished.[2] Some houses had 'double' closets, with two seats, as at Gelli Road and Bailey Street, Ton Pentre, Victoria Street and River Row, Heolfach (Ystrad), Miskin Road and Rhys Street, Trealaw, and Waun Court, Tonypandy.[3]

The need for good planning of communities and minimum standards of drainage, refuse and effluent disposal rightly became the focus of attention towards the end of the 1870s. In January 1879 the authority adopted a set of byelaws (based on a model put forward by the Local Government Board) to help them administer sanitary matters and control building development. The road to sanitary reform in the Rhondda, as elsewhere, was not without difficulties. The medical officer, Watkin Rhys, showed open hostility to other officers who appeared to be dragging their feet, reporting to a meeting in April 1879 that 'summer will possibly visit us ere long and how are we to live with filth, nastiness and stinks allowed to accumulate by your officers amongst us?'[4] Rhys's work, however, did bring the Rhondda to a point at which it was able to make some contribution towards improving sanitary standards, although for the next 50 years such activity had to cope with ceaseless immigration (and consequent mounting challenges). He at least saw, before his death in 1880, the beginnings of a new era of better sanitary conditions and most important, the adoption of the byelaws which were to dictate the form of housing development in the Rhondda throughout the next half-century.

[1] Ibid., 21 June 1878.
[2] Ibid., 22 Nov. and 6 Dec. 1878.
[3] Ibid., 17 March 1879.
[4] Ibid., 25 April 1879.

The introduction of byelaws

The byelaws came into effect on 21 August 1879.[1] They not only covered the layout of streets and buildings but also placed obligations on the occupiers of houses to clean adjoining pavements at least once a day, to clean privies, earth closets and ash pits (not to do so could lead to a penalty of £1) and to ensure the removal of household rubbish. In respect of streets, the minimum width was set at 36ft and a suitable surface, camber, kerbs and footways were required. Buildings had to conform to minimum standards of construction, including the need to have a 'proper damp course of sheet lead, asphalt, or slates laid in cement, or of other durable material impervious to moisture' and had to conform to minimum room heights and wall thicknesses. The width of stone walls had to be 'one third greater than that prescribed for a wall built of bricks', which contributed to the soundness of construction of so much of the property built in the Rhondda.

Minimum standards were set for windows and ventilation, together with an open space requirement at the rear of houses (exclusive to each dwelling) of 'an aggregate extent not less than one hundred and fifty square feet, and free from any erection therein ... except a water closet, earth closet, or privy, and an ashpit'. Water closets had to have appropriate cisterns, with arrangements for flushing and ventilation, and earth closets had to have moveable receptacles. Such closets had to be at least ten feet from the house and thirty feet from any water supplied for drinking or household purposes. Finally, and perhaps most important, the byelaws meant that plans for the development of new streets had to be submitted for approval, with the work subject to systematic inspection by surveyors.

These byelaws have left an indelible mark on the Rhondda's development, ensuring that much of the housing has a strong uniformity of character, regardless of tenure or the agency of development.

Conclusion

Colliery development and house-building prior to 1879 are clearly and closely related to each other. In the early days settlements were small and clung closely to the new pits, the housing often being provided (if only by temporary huts in some instances) by the colliery owners. The scale of development, however, was such that the rural landscape still dominated. In

---

[1] Ystradyfodwg Local Board, *Bye Laws with respect to: I. Cleansing of footways and privies, etc; II. Nuisances; III. New streets and buildings; IV. Slaughter houses* (1879).

the upper Rhondda Fawr the 'cores' of communities had been established at Tynewydd, Treherbert and Treorchy, with smaller developments at Pentre, Ton Pentre and Ystrad. Odd terraces and groups of cottages had been built at Fernhill, Blaenrhondda, Blaenycwm and Cwmparc. Lower down the valley there was a significant community at Llwynypia (essentially the 'Scotch' terraces), limited developments at Tonypandy, Trealaw, Penygraig and Dinas, and an isolated pair of terraces (Bush Houses) at Blaenclydach. The Rhondda Fach was almost completely undeveloped apart from 'core' communities at Ferndale and Blaenllechau, limited settlements at Porth, Cymmer and Trebanog, and small groups of cottages at Ynyshir.

This period, however, provided the basis on which the rapid development of the remainder of the Rhondda would take place. The houses, though simple in style, became larger and were increasingly built in terraces. In reflecting needs arising from Rhondda's growth they were establishing a model for future housing. The colliery owners, whilst initially the main providers of housing, were beginning to find that private developers, attracted by the booming local economy, were happy to take on this role.

Farms and cottages still dominated the rural hillslopes and much of the Rhondda Fach. The new settlements were established alongside a small but long-standing farming community whose way of life had changed little in several centuries. The rural nature of the Rhondda however, had been lost in some parts and would be overturned completely in the next decade.

4

The Colliery Owners

Colliery owners were concerned to get a profit from their mines and, on the whole, cared less for the living conditions of the colliers and their families. In the early period of development provision for workers was often just a row or two of huts. The fact that owners had, in some instances, only short leases for mineral rights clearly discouraged them from providing more permanent accommodation; hence the erection of 'crudely constructed wooden huts' in association with pits at Blaenycwm, Ynysfeio, Tylorstown, Ferndale and Blaenllechau.[1]

The role of the owners in the building of houses was greatest in the early years of the Rhondda's growth, especially where collieries were developed in isolated places.[2] This period was marked not only by the erection of temporary accommodation for immigrant workers and their families, but by an increasing number of permanent houses which either replaced or added to the hut 'encampments'. The tentative early schemes of Walter Coffin at Dinas and of David Davies at Ton Pentre (Ton Row, Parry Street etc) have been noted, as has the more substantial enterprise of Archibald Hood in building the 'Scotch' terraces at Llwynypia. As time progressed, the role of the owner generally diminished, although there were a few exceptions which are mentioned later. David Davies's Ocean Coal Co., which had extended its building operations to Cwmparc, decided to discontinue its role as a housing provider, stating in 1885 that:

> A colliery company has much to gain by encouraging the public to build largely in its vicinity so as to secure their keep and support in any conflict they may become involved in with their workmen ... in view of this it is worthwhile for the colliery company to do its best to encourage the public to build, even though by doing so it gives up a favourable opportunity for investing capital in a perfectly safe and very lucrative investment.[3]

---

[1] Lewis, *Rhondda Valleys*, p. 201.
[2] P.N. Jones, *Colliery settlement in the South Wales coalfield, 1850 to 1926* (Hull, 1969), pp. 38–9.
[3] Quoted in ibid., p. 47.

The profit on housing investment was said by H.S. Jevons to be less than that from mining.[1] In addition, the amount of money required to open a colliery was so great that the owner would have little incentive to invest in housing as well. Such investment was, in any case, less likely to be needed in view of the growing role of both building clubs and private developers, who were specifically concerned with housing.[2]

Further major investments by colliery owners were made in Ferndale, Tylorstown, Wattstown and later Llwyncelyn, suggesting that sufficient money could be raised and that such activity remained a profitable sideline to the working of the collieries themselves. Appendix 1 lists known colliery company housing developments and indicates particular concentrations in the upper Rhondda Fawr and in the Rhondda Fach.

The motivation for companies to build houses was not purely financial. Maerdy Colliery, for instance, was singled out by the sanitary authority for its 'commendable liberality' in providing a 'Coffee Tavern, reading room, bagatelle and billiard tables, lawn tennis ground'.[3] Philanthropy may have been a factor in some other developments. It was, however, notably absent in a number of instances when it came to putting right nuisances. In 1878 the South Wales Coal Co. tried to evade responsibility for the accumulation of liquid soil at the rear of its houses at Caroline Street, Blaenrhondda.[4] These houses, isolated at the northernmost limit of the Rhondda Fawr, had two downstairs rooms and three bedrooms, reached by a 'reversed' stair (Fig. 4.1; Plate 4). There were no rear extensions.[5]

The provision of privies was often inadequate. There were, for instance, just four for sixteen huts at Blaenrhondda owned by the Dunraven Colliery, and no privies or closets at all for the twenty cottages at Cwmgorki owned by the Abergorki Colliery Co.[6]

Some new developments were taking place. In Tylorstown, H. Tylor & Co. obtained sixteen leases from the Crawshay Bailey estate between 1877 and 1883 for a total of 93 houses in East Road and Hendrefadog Street. They also obtained a lease enabling them to extract stone from a nearby

---

[1] H.S. Jevons, *The British coal trade* (Repr. Newton Abbot, 1969), p. 645.

[2] See Chapters 5 and 6.

[3] Glamorgan Record Office, Ystradyfodwg Urban Sanitary Authority, 7 July 1882.

[4] Ibid., 16 Aug. 1878.

[5] I am indebted to Christopher Powell for permission to redraw his plans of a house in Caroline Street.

[6] GRO, Ystradyfodwg USA, 1 Aug. and 12 Sept. 1879.

FIRST FLOOR.

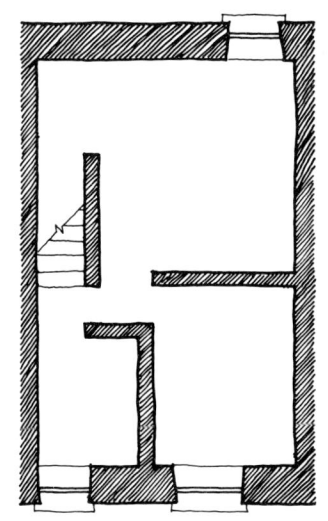

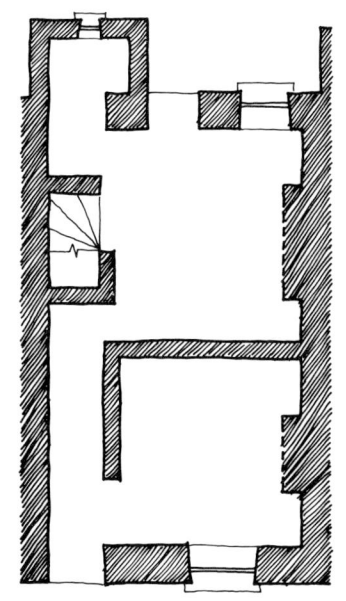

GROUND FLOOR.

4.1 Caroline Street, Blaenrhondda

quarry.[1] The properties, such as 5 East Road (Fig. 4.2; Plate 5), are double-fronted with two downstairs and two upstairs rooms. All have roofs of imported slate and many have only a narrow yard at the rear (in which the privy and coal store are situated), bounded by a high retaining wall with steps leading to 'mountainside' gardens. Their simplicity and size had much in common with the earlier period of the Rhondda's development.

In 1884 the National Steam Coal Co. obtained a lease for the building of 60 houses at Hillside Terrace, Wattstown. The lease was for 99 years at an annual ground rent of £45, with a requirement to insure for £6,000 (i.e. a ground rent for each house of 15s and a value for insurance purposes of £100). A mortgage was raised for the development through the Welsh Economic Building Society.[2] The properties are single-fronted and, being built after byelaws had been introduced, have much in common with most later Rhondda terraced houses. An example is 31 Hillside Terrace (Fig. 4.3). This incorporates a rear scullery extension (a feature that was now becoming a standard addition to local houses) and, though stone-built, the walls are rendered. There is a 'reversed' stairway from the living room (more common in the earlier period of industrial development) giving access to three upstairs bedrooms, a layout which created an enclosed small landing area without natural light. The same company obtained a further lease for 39 more houses in Hillside Terrace and Bailey Street, Wattstown, on 1 June 1885, which were built to the same design.

After 1890 the role of the colliery owners in the provision of housing diminished. They had mixed feelings about building houses, especially as greater demands were placed on them by a local authority that was increasingly willing to exercise its new powers concerning the supply of water for household consumption and flushing closets, and the provision of adequate drainage. In 1890 the medical officer of health reported that 100 houses owned by D. Davis & Son at Ferndale and Blaenllechau were without drains or a water supply.[3] There were, in addition, repeated reports of unsatisfactory conditions at the Concrete Houses, Dinas (which were built of rubble in a cement matrix), owned by Dinas Steam Colliery Co. (Plate 6).[4] Insanitary conditions were also in evidence at the 'Scotch' terraces, Llwynypia, where a growing lack of interest by the owners (the Glamorgan)

---

[1] Crawshay Bailey estate records in private hands (Hendrefadog Farm register). The first two leases to Tylor were for the erection of huts. The quarry was where the Duke of York public house now stands.

[2] Crawshay Bailey estate records (Tir Bach Farms and Aberllechau Farms registers).

[3] GRO, Ystradyfodwg Local Board, 16 May 1890.

[4] GRO, Ystradyfodwg USA, 9 June 1882; Local Board, 18 Sept. 1891.

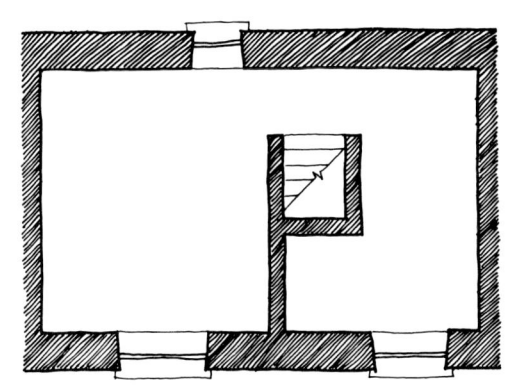

FIRST FLOOR.

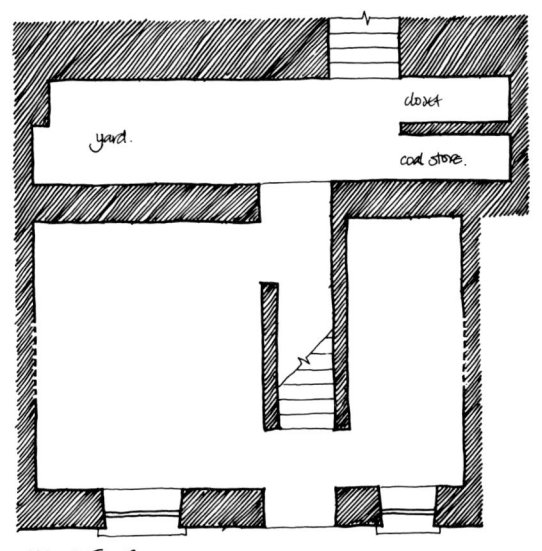

yard.
closet
coal store.

GROUND FLOOR.

0   5   10 FEET.

4.2 5 East Road, Tylorstown

FIRST FLOOR

coal store   closet

GROUND FLOOR

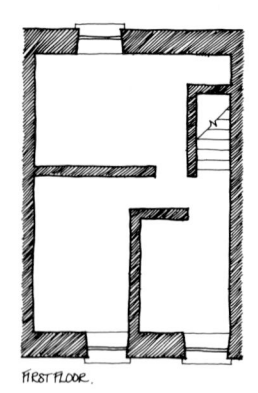

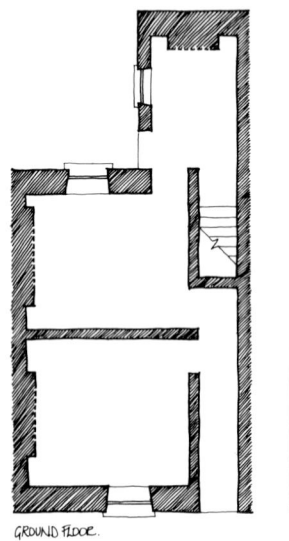

4.3 31 Hillside Terrace, Wattstown

Colliery Co.) perhaps indicated the fact that they were selling many of the houses to sitting tenants.[1]

This ambivalent attitude meant that improvements to company houses were sometimes only achieved by compromise. The Cymmer Colliery Co., for example, paid £130 to the sanitary authority to help fund the conversion of ash closets to water closets at its houses.[2] In other cases, such as the Cambrian Colliery Co.'s houses at Marion Street, Clydach Vale, there was lengthy and bitter correspondence with the authority over the company's failure to comply with notices to put right nuisances caused by 'structural and other defects'.[3] This exchange came shortly after the Cambrian Combine's dispute with its workers (the Cambrian 'lockout') which may well explain the company's lack of concern.

Although most new building by colliery companies had stopped, a notable exception was the Lewis Merthyr Consolidated Collieries Ltd, which built what amounted almost to a new village between 1890 and 1902: 214 houses at Llwyncelyn, an area where it has been argued that company housing was unnecessary.[4] This development is of interest in that it has three-bedroomed houses as standard but every fourth house has an additional bedroom above a substantially built rear extension, as at 4 Nythbrân Terrace (Fig. 4.4). Although the layout is broadly conventional, in this case the turned stair is omitted in favour of two half-landings.

Other smaller developments in this later period include those by the United National Collieries of 40 houses at Pleasant View, Wattstown, and by D. Davis & Son of ten houses at Middle Terrace, Stanleytown.[5] Davis's Ferndale Coal Co. also demolished and rebuilt their 55 wooden huts at Blaenllechau during 1906-08, substituting 'one-storey brick buildings, little larger in character and containing in comparison with the old houses a third bedroom, as well as a pantry and with a scullery'.[6] Some of the houses, whose total reconstruction cost was about £7,000, are shown in Plate 7. The activity of Davis and other companies in this period contrasted with the tardiness of a decade before, leading the medical officer to commend them

---

[1] GRO, Ystradyfodwg Local Board, 13 July 1900; M.J. Daunton, 'Miners' housing: South Wales and the Great Northern Coalfield, 1880–1914', *International Review of Social History*, 25 (1980), 150.

[2] GRO, Ystradyfodwg Local Board, 23 Sept. 1902 and 12 June 1903.

[3] RUDC, RMOH 1900.

[4] P.N. Jones, 'Aspects of the population and settlement geography of the South Wales coalfield' (Birmingham University Ph.D. thesis, 1965), p. 310.

[5] Crawshay Bailey estate records (Tir Bach, Aberllechau and Penyrheol registers).

[6] RUDC, RMOH 1906, 1908.

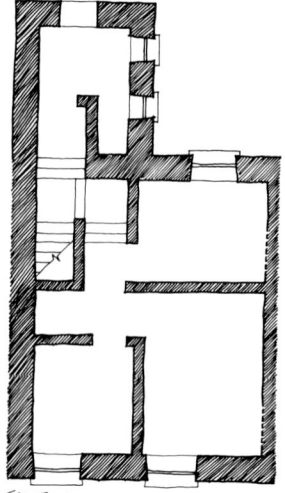

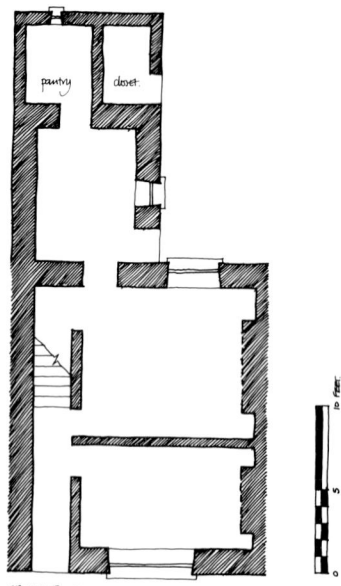

4.4 Nythbrân Terrace, Llwyncelyn

for their 'promptitude' in undertaking repairs when called upon to do so by the authority.[1]

Conclusion

One argument put forward to justify house-building by colliery owners is concerned with social control and suggests that workers 'tied' to their employment would be more dependent on their employer and more compliant.[2] This may have been true in other coalfields, or earlier in the nineteenth century, but does not appear to be the case in the Rhondda. The contrary can, in fact, be argued: that a house owner is more tied to his location (and job) than the tenant of a company house. Indeed, during a stoppage affecting the South Dunraven Colliery at Blaenrhondda in 1894, some 30 colliery houses were found to be empty after two weeks of the dispute and 46 after a month, suggesting that miners and their families were quite prepared to abandon their tenancies to seek work elsewhere.[3]

For the companies, house-building offered an economic rate of return. The Glamorgan Coal Co.'s rents for houses at Llwynypia valued at £80 each were between 16s and 17s a month in 1908. Other houses of the same age valued at £180 yielded only £1 6s, which shows that, where housing was provided, rents were set at market levels.[4] The colliery owners played a role in housing development that was significant to begin with but then diminished, probably because of an increasing reluctance (with some notable exceptions) to build in accordance with the higher standards of sanitation required (and increasingly enforced) by the local authority after the adoption of byelaws in 1879. The limited later role of the companies belies the widespread assumption that the Rhondda followed the pattern found in other coalfields.[5] The contrary must be emphasised—namely that the Rhondda's development was so rapid, and the activities of building clubs and private speculators (discussed in Chapters 5 and 6) so great, that the need for companies to build houses in large numbers was simply not there.

---

[1] RUDC, RMOH 1912.
[2] Jones, *Colliery settlement*, p. 46.
[3] Ibid.
[4] Daunton, 'Miners' houses', p. 150.
[5] The assumption that miners in the Rhondda (and elsewhere in South Wales) were invariably tenants of the colliery companies needs to be firmly refuted, since the importance of building clubs and private speculators was a fundamental characteristic that distinguishes the region from, e.g., the Scottish and North Eastern coalfields.

5

Building Clubs

Almost forgotten among house-building agencies in the Rhondda are the building clubs. These were responsible for about a quarter of the houses built in the central valleys of the coalfield after 1878 and an unknown proportion before this date. They were, however, far less important in Cardiff, where speculative building predominated.[1] The building club's role in the coalfield varied according to prevailing economic conditions and the activity of other agencies. They were particularly active for a short period in the late 1850s and intermittently to the 1880s, after which they operated very successfully until shortly before the First World War. Clubs were most prominent during the periods of greatest building activity generally and on the upswings of cycles when incomes would be relatively high (and secure) and money could be borrowed easily.[2]

Each club was an association of potential home owners who collectively obtained mortgages and other loans to pay for the building of their houses. Eventually, the club would be dissolved and each member would become an owner (normally with the benefit of his own mortgage). To add a certain authority to the club, local professional people (solicitors, accountants etc) were invited to become shareholders. The origin of the clubs is obscure. There were terminating building societies in the Midlands from *c*. 1775 and building clubs in Lancashire from the late 1780s.[3] In South Wales the earliest known building club or building society development, at 'Club Row', Abersychan, was completed around 1840, although there is a possibility that clubs were operating considerably earlier than this and Jevons suggested that

---

[1] M.J. Daunton, *Coal Metropolis. Cardiff 1870–1914* (Leicester, 1977), p. 96.

[2] Daunton, 'Miners' houses', p. 150. I am indebted to J.H. Richards of the Centre for Population Studies at Cardiff for his observations on building club activity in relation to building cycles.

[3] M.H. Yeadall, 'Building societies in the West Riding of Yorkshire and their contribution to housing provision in the nineteenth century' in M. Doughty (ed.), *Building the industrial city* (Leicester, 1986), p. 59; I am indebted to Mr W.J. Smith for information on building clubs in Lancashire.

the system was imported from Yorkshire.[1] A survey undertaken in 1849–51 notes of Merthyr Tydfil that the working man 'in numerous instances ... buys and builds his own house (not by the aid of Building Societies) but with his own proper and ready means', which suggests that even if clubs were not active the pre-conditions for their success were present.[2]

Building clubs were similar to terminating building societies. In the latter savers and borrowers were identical: each member saved a regular amount which was lent to the individual members as and when enough was available. The order of borrowing was normally determined by ballot. When each member had obtained a loan the society (as is clear from its title) was wound up. The establishment of 'permanent' building societies (and a new Act in 1874 which made balloting for advances illegal) effectively killed off the older type of society in Yorkshire,[3] but this did not happen in South Wales, even though building societies had been established. In 1871 *Kelly's South Wales Directory* lists agencies and offices in Pontypridd for the Bristol & West of England Building Society and the Pontypridd, Llantrisant & Rhondda Valleys Benefit Building Society. The clubs continued to flourish, perhaps offering particular benefits that met the local circumstances of the Rhondda and other valley communities.

Modus operandi

Since building clubs, like terminating building societies, were only temporary, little information about them survives. We know, however, that they operated on a share basis, one share being equal to the cost of building a house plus a small sum to cover administrative overheads. Each member made a down-payment which, together with money from local banks, enabled an advance to be paid to a contractor. The members then paid on a monthly basis. There was also a system of penalties which encouraged members not to get into arrears. A member could hold more than one share.

The rules of the Victoria Building Club in nearby Caerphilly, which appears to have been established in 1902, are probably typical.[4] These

---

[1] J. Lowe, *Welsh industrial workers' housing, 1775–1875* (Cardiff, 1977), p. 47; the development was undertaken by the Pentwyn Benefit Building Society, established in 1838. Jevons, *Coal Trade*, p. 646, offers no evidence for his claim concerning the Yorkshire origins of South Wales building clubs.

[2] Ginswick (ed.), *Labour and the poor*, p. 56.

[3] Yeadall, 'Building societies', p. 70.

[4] Glamorgan Record Office, Rules of the Victoria Building Club, Caerphilly.

include the requirement for each member to make a down-payment of £5 and a subscription of 10s per lunar month. Arrears of eight weeks resulted in a fine of 6d, with a fine of 1s 6d after twelve weeks and 6d per month thereafter. A member who was nine months in arrears would be required to sell his share to a person approved by the trustees. The figures for payments are similar to those noted elsewhere, which in the 1900s might be anything from 10s to 25s per month, a sizeable proportion of the wages of most working men at the time.[1] Such payments were sufficient to enable the raising of individual mortgages and the paying off of any residual interest and capital sums (thereby allowing the dissolution of the club) within a period of 15 to 25 years. In practice it appears that building clubs in the Rhondda were, on the whole, terminated more quickly, although the general point is still valid.

The trustees of a building club would normally be ordinary members appointed by their fellows. They would arrange the necessary loans and hold the land and buildings on behalf of the club, which would own the houses until all debts and liabilities had been paid and the club could be wound up.[2] Each member could occupy his house on completion, the order of occupation normally being determined by lot.[3] In certain cases however, allocation was determined by housing need and possibly, on occasion, by payment of a premium.[4] No member could hold their own deeds until the winding-up of the club.

The size of club developments in the Rhondda varied from seven to 111 houses (see Appendix 2), the duration of the club being determined chiefly by the number of properties, the size of the monthly payments and the amount of money raised. Hardship following strikes, lockouts or pit disasters would result in an extension of the life of a club, due to a temporary drop in income. A further consideration would be the state of the money market which could precipitate or delay winding-up, depending on whether individual mortgages could be obtained at favourable rates.

The rules of building clubs were drawn up, as far as possible, to ensure

---

[1] Jevons, *Coal trade*, pp. 646–7. Significantly higher figures are given just five years later in the *Report of the South Wales Regional Survey Committee* (Ministry of Health, 1920).

[2] In the case of the Victoria Building Club winding-up could not take place until liabilities were reduced to £100 per share, disbanding being a matter for a decision at a general meeting. Jevons, *Coal trade*, p. 647, noted that clubs disbanded when about one-fourth of the cost of each house had been paid.

[3] Jevons, *Coal trade*, p. 647. It appears that such building clubs fells outside the scope of the Building Societies Act 1874 which precluded such lotteries. The rules of the Victoria Building Club specify that it was to be 'unregistered', as no doubt were other clubs.

[4] I am indebted to J.H. Richards for this observation.

fairness for all members. The houses were invariably terraced and simple in form. Thus a rule for the Abergwynfi No 1 Building Club (in the upper Afan valley) included a clause specifying that all houses 'shall be erected according to one and the same plan and specification, and in the same style', although in other instances it appears that provision was made for members to pay extra for an additional bedroom.[1]

After the formation of a club it was commonplace for their role to be extended and for plans to be drawn up for further developments. Various examples are given in Appendix 2, such as the Pentre Building Club which submitted schemes in 1888, 1890 and 1892. In other cases new building clubs would be formed on the dissolution of the first, which would probably retain the services of some of the trustees and raise money from the same sources. An example may well be the Wattstown Building Club established in 1896 which, following dissolution and reconstitution, submitted further plans in 1909.

Some examples

The character of club developments in the Rhondda was in keeping with houses built by others. A typical club development was that at Redfield Street, Ystrad (Fig. 5.1). This club, established in 1884, built 26 three-bedroomed houses in traditional style, with a parlour, living room, scullery and small pantry. The first floor is reached by a straight stair, turned at the top. The sandstone walls are 'dressed' at the front. The ground floor is laid with flagstones and the roof slated.

The lease for these building club properties was in the names of the trustees, Thomas Thomas, a provision merchant, and Jonathan Rees, a colliery overman. It was granted on 20 May 1884 but surrendered just five years later, when each shareholder was issued with his own lease, dated 3 June 1889, for 99 years from 1 November 1884. A ground rent of £1 1s per annum was payable on each property and the leaseholder was required to insure his house for £140.[2]

The following list gives the trades and occupation of the club members, some of whom held more than one share so that they could rent out any additional houses which they eventually owned:

---

[1] Jones, *Colliery settlement*, p. 44.
[2] Crawshay Bailey estate records, Melin yr Hom and Gelligaled farm registers.

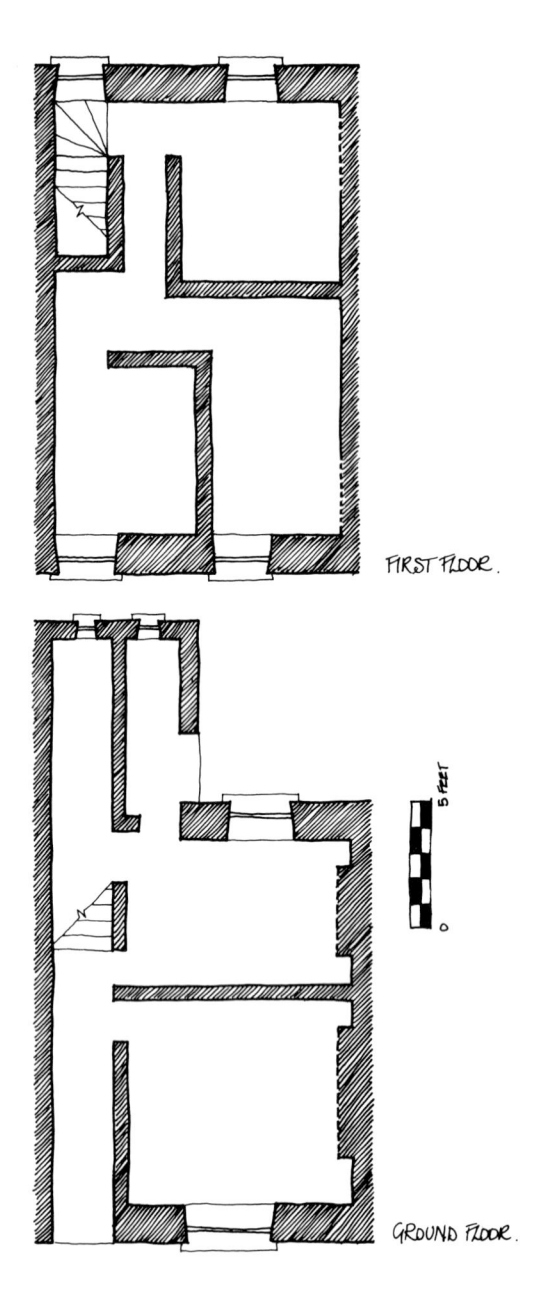

5.1 3 Redfield Street, Ystrad

David Davies, Butter Merchant
William Griffiths, Collier
Thomas Jenkins, Mason
John Butler, Butcher
William Thomas, Collier
David Jenkins, Builder (two shares)
Jonathan Rees, Colliery Overman (Trustee)
Obadiah Llewellyn, Rate Collector
Thomas Thomas, Provisions Merchant (8 shares, Trustee)
John Davies, Collier
Rees Llewellyn, Colliery Overman
William Morgan, Hotel Keeper
Evan Richards, Engineer
John Davies, Innkeeper
William White, Collier
Daniel Thomas, Timberman
William John Thomas, Collier

Other clubs had a similar variety of trades among their members and, on the whole, sought to develop similar terraced properties. Their role, therefore, was somewhat different from that of the terminating building societies which, in Yorkshire, were 'not for the ordinary labourer. Rather they were for the upper working class or the lower middle class wanting to move out of their way'.[1] Some clubs in the Rhondda did build to a higher standard and may have been trying to satisfy upper working-class aspirations. Llyn Crescent, Ferndale, for instance, is a club development of thirteen terraced properties with bay windows and higher than normal space standards (Fig. 5.2; Plate 8). The traditional half-hall is absent; instead a full hall gives direct access to the rear scullery without any need to pass through the living room. The substantially built rear extension allows for a third upstairs bedroom—the main body of the house being larger than normal.

Leases were granted by the Crawshay Bailey estate for Llyn Crescent in 1909 to Francis Henry Reece, a wagon builder of 22 Rhondda Terrace, Edward Jones, a miner of 6 Fountain Street, William Meyrick, an engine driver of 6 Darren Terrace, and John Jenkins, a miner of 5 Rhondda Terrace.[2] These men acted on behalf of the club, the lease being

taken up by the Assignors ... for and on behalf of the Assignee and

---

[1] Yeadall, 'Building societies', p. 61.

[2] Crawshay Bailey estate records, Duffryn Saffrwch register.

54　　　　　　　　　BUILDING CLUBS

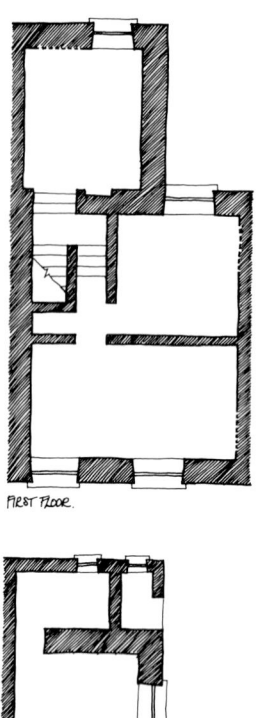

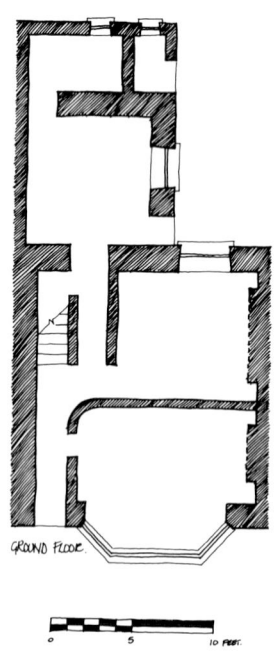

FIRST FLOOR.

GROUND FLOOR.

0   5   10 FEET

5.2　8 Llyn Terrace, Ferndale

other persons being members of a Voluntary Association formed and constituted on the twenty sixth day of October one thousand nine hundred and eight under the name of the Llyn Crescent Building Club, Ferndale.

Leases were individually assigned in 1914: that for 8 Llyn Crescent to John Jenkins, a pit carpenter, and those for numbers 10, 9 and 7 to Messrs Rees, Jones and Jenkins respectively. Each property was subject to an annual ground rent of £1 15s. Individual mortgage arrangements are not known for all club members, but it is interesting to note that in 1914 five loans were provided by Rhondda Urban District Council under the 1899 Small Dwellings Acquisition Act for between £200 and £208, to be repaid within 15 years at 4 per cent interest.[1] The beneficiaries were Mary Jane Meyrick at No 1, Hugh Thomas Hughes at No 2, Daniel James Williams at No 3, Jenkin Jones at No 8, and John William Evans at No 13. Jenkin Jones's repayments were £1 10s 10d per month.[2]

The 1899 Act was used extensively by the council and may, in several cases, have helped building clubs to terminate during the difficult period at the outbreak of war. That building clubs were still active at this time is testimony to the importance of their role in the Rhondda through the whole period of development.

Conclusion

Building clubs were active throughout the period from the mid-nineteenth century to the Great War. From 1900 to 1911 they were responsible for at least 36 per cent of the plans submitted for local authority approval in Rhondda Fach and at least 15 per cent in Rhondda Fawr. In the previous decade they were responsible for 23 per cent of housing in the Rhondda as a whole.[3]

---

[1] RUDC Finance Committee, 28 July 1914.

[2] Deeds to 8 Llyn Crescent, courtesy Mr and Mrs J. Williams.

[3] Daunton, 'Miners' houses', p. 147. Daunton notes that house plans submitted by building clubs in the Rhondda represent 23% and 18% of all plans in the periods 1889–99 and 1900–11 respectively. This compares with 37% and 58% in Merthyr Tydfil and 0.4% and 44% in Llantrisant & Llantwit Fardre in approximately the same periods. In 1910–14 72% of the plans submitted in Merthyr Tydfil were from building clubs. The figures for the Rhondda are likely to underestimate the true position, since some plans were submitted in the names of trustees and may not have been recognised as coming from a club. In Pontypridd 11% and 18% of plans for the periods in question were submitted by clubs.

Building clubs, it has been suggested, were at this time peculiar to South Wales, their continued existence 'possibly only in the type of society and with the range of social attitudes found in the valleys', where voluntarism, co-operation and social cohesion were unusually strong.[1] We might add to this the importance of the nonconformist chapels in promoting values of community endeavour; the common working and living experience of local people; and the development of the labour movement and socialist beliefs. This argument should not be taken too far. There are no clubs in the Rhondda bearing the names of chapels and only one with possible political connections, the Cymru Fydd Building Club, bearing the title of the movement for a Welsh parliament active in the late nineteenth century.

There was, at the same time, no significant middle class in the Rhondda (or in the Valleys as a whole) which might have invested in private rented housing. With the reluctance of colliery owners to provide houses, and with fewer middle class investors than in other industrial communities, the building clubs were able to play a major role.

The decline of the clubs only came with the collapse of the private housing market in the years immediately preceding the outbreak of war. In 1915 H.S. Jevons noted that 'owing to the widespread depreciation of property in recent years fewer guarantors are now available, which may be one cause of the decreased building by this method in South Wales'.[2] The suggestion that the club system had been 'breaking up' for 'many years before the war' is not true in the Rhondda where new clubs were being set up as late as 1914. Similarly, the allegation that 'certain political and trade union interests had much to do with the breakdown of this form of enterprise' is only plausible in so far as the increasing conflict between colliery owners and their workers acted as a disincentive to potential investors.[3]

The demise of building clubs was due to a mixture of factors, including increases in building costs (notably for materials) and the vulnerable economy of the South Wales coalfield, both of which affected the whole of the housing market and are discussed in Chapter 8.

---

[1] Daunton, *Coal metropolis*, p. 111.
[2] Jevons, *Coal trade*, p. 647.
[3] Ministry of Health, *Report of the South Wales Regional Survey Committee* (1920), p. 28.

6

Private Developers, Investors and other Providers of Housing

One of the factors relieving colliery owners of the need to build houses was the active role of speculative investors alongside building clubs. The term 'speculative investor' includes both private investors and speculative builders erecting houses for sale or rent, the latter being the more important agency in the Rhondda. Speculative builders would erect houses mostly for sale, although some might be retained for rent at certain times, e.g. in a period of declining house prices.[1] They would use money from the sale of houses to raise new mortgages to fund further building and also acted as contractors for other agencies, e.g. building clubs. The activities of speculative builders, it has been suggested, may have been greater in leasehold areas, such as the Rhondda, since they did not need to buy land outright.[2] Private investors, on the other hand, were mainly concerned with building houses to rent. While many would buy directly from speculative builders, others, as noted in the last chapter, would buy multiple shareholdings in building clubs. Either way, it was clear that the ownership of houses to rent was considered a sound investment offering a reasonable return.

The quality of houses put up by speculative builders varied, the best incorporating higher space standards, more substantial rear extensions, bay windows etc, and being generally sold for owner occupation. The worst, by contrast, were built to the minimum allowable standards and frequently included separate cellar dwellings and basements. This reflected the difficulty of obtaining suitable sites and the fact that considerable 'cutting and filling' was often necessary. A separate cellar dwelling, though humble and often without adequate ventilation or natural light, provided a greater financial return (either by sale or rental) to compensate for the extra work involved. The standards of building often left much to be desired. In 1916 it was argued that 'the planning of mining villages has been left entirely to landowners and speculators whose object has been to obtain as large a return

---

[1] H. Richards, 'The demographic factor', in H. Richards (ed.), *Population and factor movements in economic development* (Cardiff, 1976), p. 198.

[2] M. Doughty (ed.), *Building the industrial city* (Leicester, 1986), p. 10.

as possible for the least amount of expenditure ... dwellings have been crowded on the land with complete disregard for public health'.[1]

The importance of private investment in the Rhondda is reflected in the fact that some 16,000 houses were built by contractors between 1881 and 1914. These mostly had five small rooms and were erected at a cost of between £120 and £140. The rent was 4s to 5s per week.[2] The extent of private investment was largely dictated by changing economic conditions that influenced the availability of mortgages and other loans for builders or potential home owners. It has been argued that a direct link existed between average colliery wages and potential house-building activity. The prospects for private investment were generally good for the whole period of the Rhondda's development, despite economic fluctuations affecting South Wales as a whole. As J.H. Richards argued, the local housing market was always a favourite of the small investor. Rent could be obtained even in the most severe depressions, whereas yields from other investments often ceased to arrive at times of economic uncertainty. Interest rates fluctuated but the 'sticky' nature of rents assured the investor of a money income that remained fairly steady.[3]

A further factor that helped to maintain income levels from rented property (and helped households to keep up mortgage payments) was the common practice of taking in lodgers or letting out part of the house as 'rooms' or 'apartments', often to young married couples. Indeed, the constant demand from single men for lodgings close to their work acted as a cushion against fluctuating earnings from mining. This, together with the letting of rooms, would give householders the confidence and security to seek mortgages or to join building clubs.

Despite the attractions of investing in rented housing, the role of private landlords in the Rhondda remained relatively small. In the 1880s, for instance, by far the largest proportion of owners with more than one property had just three or four houses. In two wards (out of five) for which records are available, just eight people owned ten or more properties, one of whom was a local builder, Alban Richards of Ystrad Road, Pentre, who owned 15 houses. Other investors included David Thomas of Ceridwen Cottage, Ystrad, who owned houses in River Row, Ystrad, Victoria Street and Tyntyla Road, Heolfach (Ystrad), and Thomas Williams of the White Hart Inn,

---

[1] T. Richards, 'The improvement of colliery districts', *Welsh Housing Yearbook* (1917), p. 77.

[2] Lewis, *Rhondda Valleys*, p. 202.

[3] J.H. Richards, 'Fluctuations in housebuilding in the South Wales coalfield 1851–1954' (Unpublished University of Wales [Cardiff] M.A. thesis, 1956), p. 189.

Tonypandy, who owned houses in nearby Court Street and in Trealaw.[1]

Developments by speculative builders

Invariably, the houses erected by speculative builders were terraced, frequently, in rows of 20 or more. An example of such development is that by John James in Gelli, who between 1882 and 1887 built 58 properties for sale and rent in Gelli Road and Tŷ Isaf Road. These were built in groups of four or five for which 15 separate leases were obtained from the ground landlords.[2] The work was funded by a series of mortgages. No 138 Gelli Road is typical of these properties (Fig. 6.1), which were double-fronted with a through passage leading from the front to the back door. The rear extension was a slightly later addition, reached only after going out of the house into the back yard. The passage arrangement is unusual for a double-fronted property, as is the location of the stair in a corner of the living room.

Another development by a speculative builder is Brown Street (formerly Victoria Street), Ferndale, built in 1897–8 by Thomas Owen Brown, for which ten separate leases were granted.[3] Brown is perhaps best known for developing 'Brownstown' on the hillside above Tylorstown, in which the streets were named after members of his family (Cassie, Eric, Keith and Donald), which was demolished in the 1960s. 10 Brown Street (Fig. 6.2) is built to a typical Rhondda pattern, except for the lengthy rear extension, which offers a short 'bridge' to a garden at first floor level (over the ground floor pantry and closet), and also provides an additional bedroom. This particular feature is repeated in two other Brown Street properties.

Higher quality developments by speculative builders included part of Sherwood Street, Llwynypia (Fig. 6.3; Plate 9), which had substantial two-storey rear extensions and bay windows. This development was successful in attracting owner occupiers with good incomes.[4]

---

[1] Glamorgan Record Office, Ystradyfodwg Local Board, Registers of Owners and Property and Proxies for Wards 2 and 3 (1879–89). Alban Richards became a substantial figure in the Rhondda and was involved in many building developments up to the 1920s. His last contract is believed to have been the building of Hendrefadog School, Tylorstown.

[2] Crawshay Bailey estate records (Gelli Farm).

[3] Ibid. (Duffryn Saffrwch Farm).

[4] I am told by the occupant, Mrs Edna Richardson, that the street was known as 'Piano Street', reflecting the propensity of the residents to display such symbols of their affluence—no doubt visible through the bays.

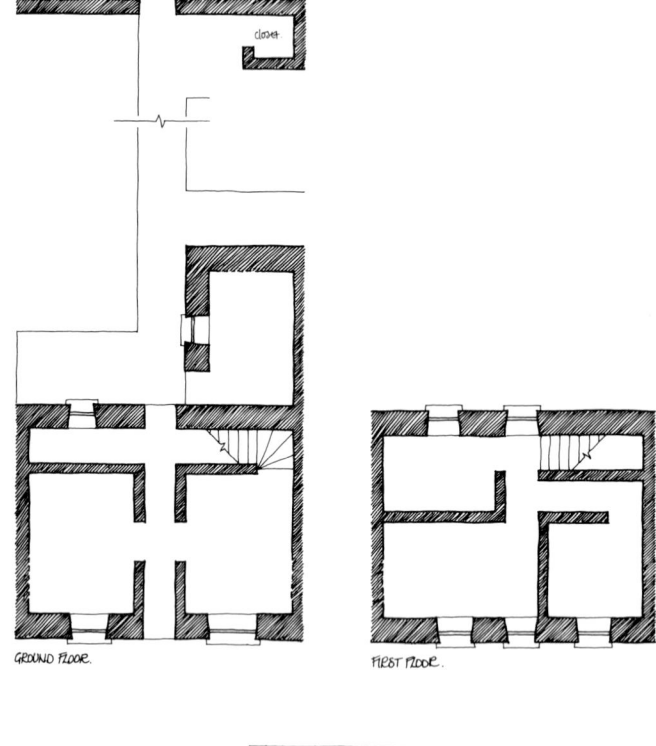

6.1 138 Gelli Road, Gelli

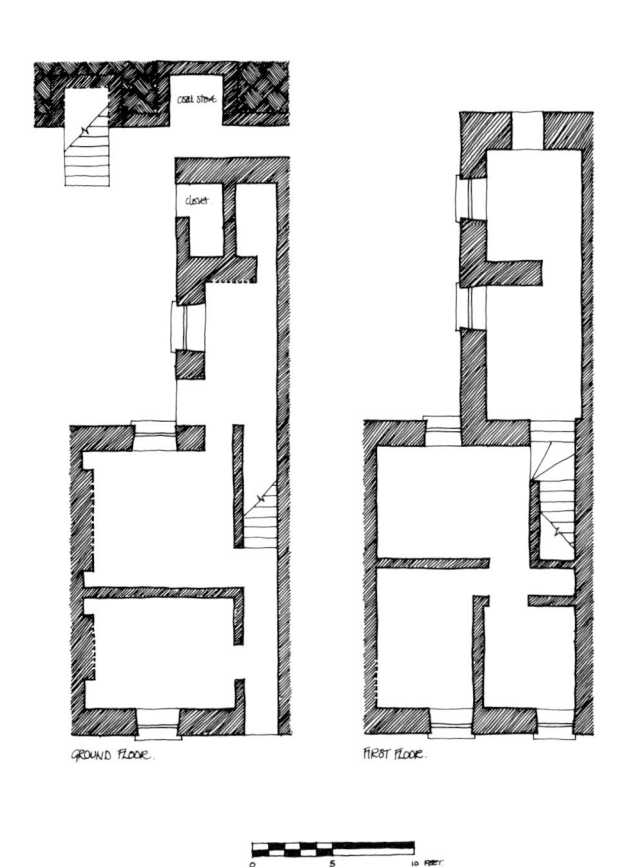

6.2 10 Brown Street, Ferndale

GROUND FLOOR.

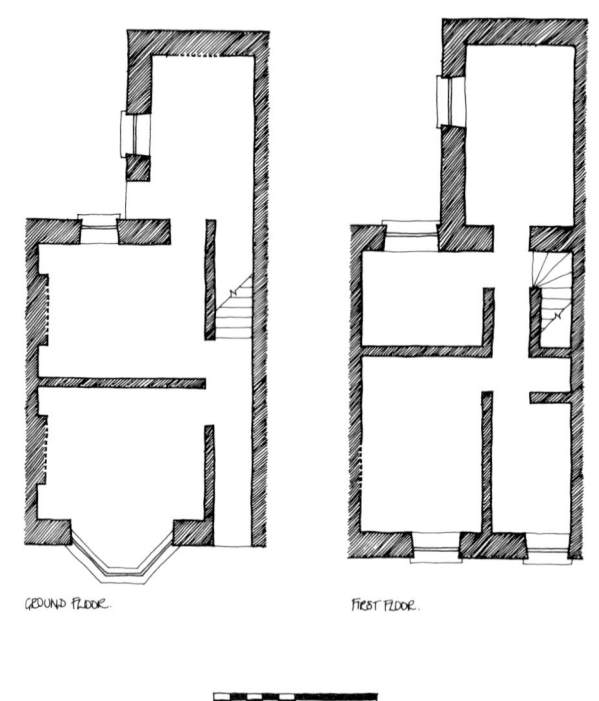

FIRST FLOOR.

6.3 43 Sherwood Street, Llwynypia

Private investors

Private investors tended to operate on a smaller scale than speculative builders and would, on the whole, simply have bought properties individually in order to offer them for rent. Where contractors were employed to build for an investor the amount of capital required to be raised would in any case have precluded large developments. Small developments by a private investor would have included the building of a house for his and his family's sole occupation, sometimes together with other houses for rent or possibly sale. The house types created in this way are, therefore, more varied, and the uniformity associated with developments by speculative builders, clubs and companies, is generally absent.

The good return on investment that helped the Rhondda's building industry maintain its momentum over half a century has been noted, as has the tendency for speculative builders to erect houses on what were often very unfavourable sites. In many areas, however, there was little alternative if housing was to be provided locally and, in any case, there were considerable numbers of miners who travelled to work from outside the Rhondda, using special workmens' trains.[1]

The problem of cellar dwellings

Many speculative builders erected houses with cellar dwellings beneath them. Such dwellings were a major concern for the local authority, since they could often be entered only from the rear and had little provision for through ventilation. Earlier developments were, in many cases, simply 'back to earth' as at 35 Commercial Street, Blaenllechau, a property with two floors below ground level (Fig. 6.4). This cellar dwelling offered a kitchen and bedroom on the lower level with a spiral stone stair leading to two bedrooms (one reached through the other) on the upper storey. An example of a cellar dwelling on one level is 37 Marion Street, Clydach Vale (Fig. 6.5), consisting of a kitchen, pantry and two bedrooms. The accommodation, though small, offered through ventilation via a narrow gap facing a substantial retaining wall to the rear.

Three-storey dwellings with basement rooms were also a cause for concern on account of the lack of light and ventilation, especially where all the rooms were used as living accommodation. An example, probably built by a private speculator, is 137 Miskin Road, Trealaw (Fig. 6.6), a street with

---

[1] Jones, *Colliery settlement*, pp. 26–7.

6.4 Under 35 Commercial Street, Blaenllechau

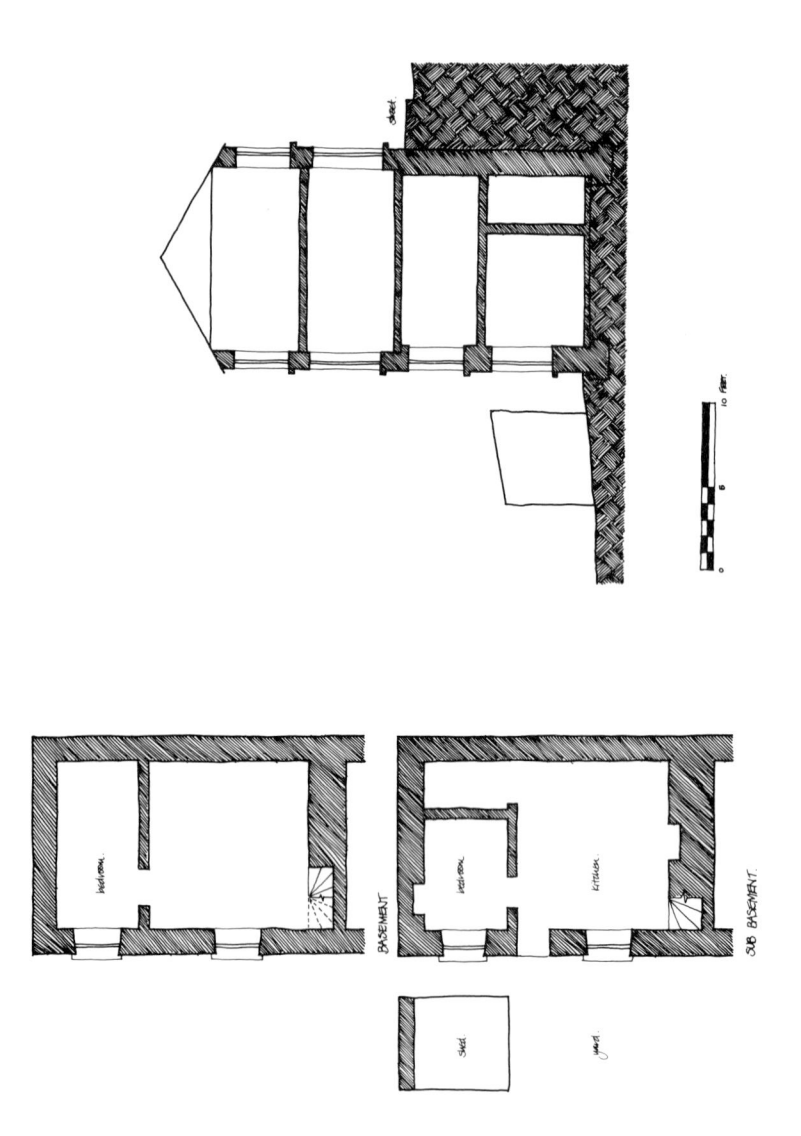

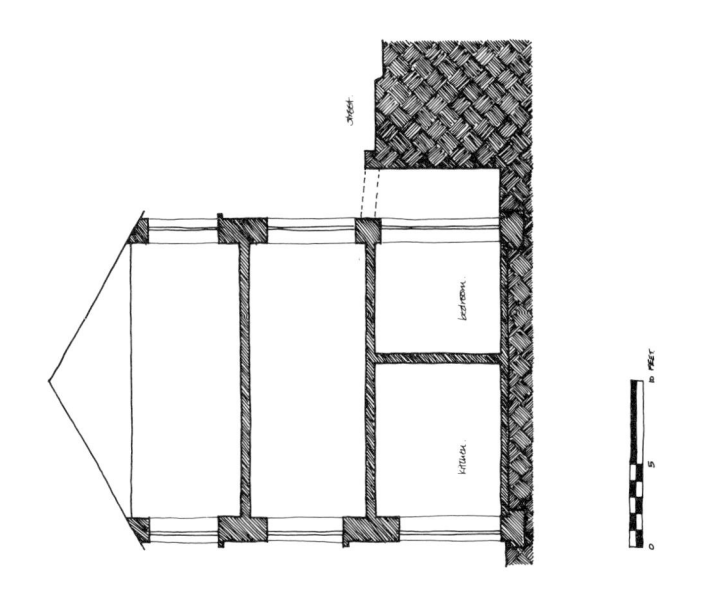

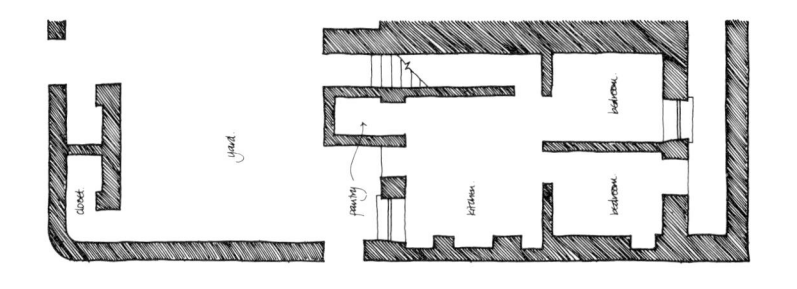

6.5 Under 37 Marion Street, Clydach Vale

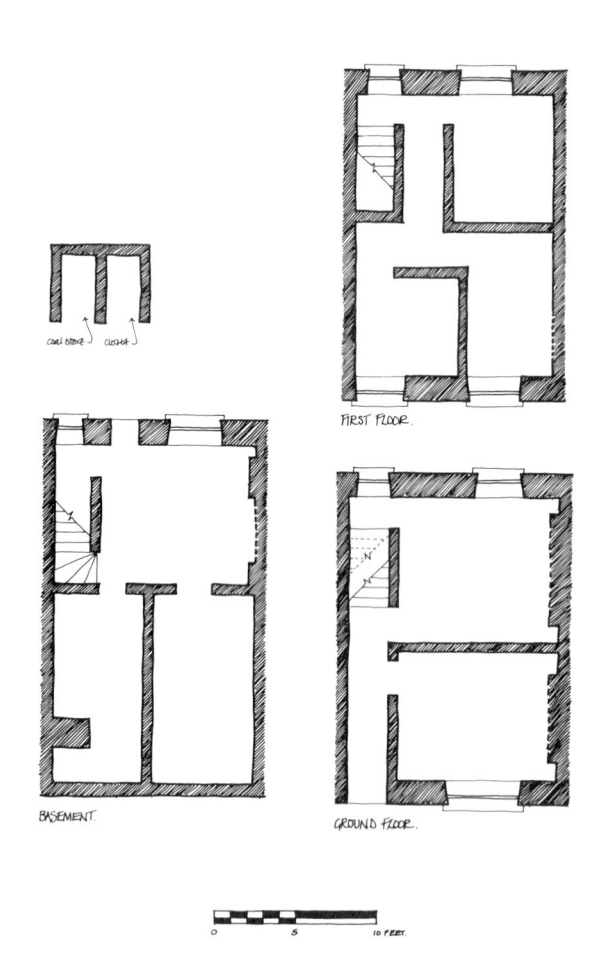

6.6 137 Miskin Road, Trealaw

many properties that attracted the attention of the local authority due to their poor sanitary conditions.

The number of separate cellar dwellings that were occupied in the Rhondda in 1899 was 548, nearly 3 per cent of the total housing stock. The highest numbers were in Gelli, Ystrad, Trealaw and Ferndale. The medical officer of health regarded none of them as fit to be inhabited, viewing the failure of the authority to take action to close the offending dwellings as a result of the still considerable housing need in the area.[1]

Other private sector problems

The problems attributed to the private sector were not confined to the insanitary conditions of many cellar dwellings or basement rooms. Builders, it is clear, bought and held sites in advance of development and because of this (and the general scarcity of building land in the Rhondda) it became increasingly difficult for other agencies (notably building clubs) to operate.

The Pentre & District Trades & Labour Council made representations to the urban district council in 1911 and, amongst other issues, drew attention to the problem of land 'monopolies'. They noted that 'the practice of builders and speculators in monopolising and bespeaking land for building purposes has been a very sore point ... insomuch as workingmen are ousted and debarred from obtaining suitable sites'.[2] The problem was acknowledged by the local authority although they offered no ideas as to how to change matters. With regard to private landlords the trades and labour council were more damning. They noted:

(a) significant rises in rents, including the example of a cottage rent being raised from 16s to 24s per month on change of ownership (with no repairs or improvements having been undertaken);
(b) that the system of 'key money' was still practised whereby the highest bidder became the tenant on payments often as high as 20s or 30s per house; and
(c) that for some houses owned by tradespeople, the tenants were required to buy at the landlord's shops, non-compliance with which often resulted in increased rents or eviction.

---

[1] RUDC, RMOH 1899 and 1900.
[2] RUDC Special Health Committee, 30 June 1911.

The medical officer, in considering these points, accepted the problem of rent increases and condemned the practice whereby tenants had to buy from particular shops. He noted that some such landlords preferred tenants with larger families and who would, therefore, have to spend more on provisions.[1]

Conclusion

By 1910 the Rhondda had nearly reached its peak in terms of both housing development and population. Demand for housing was at its highest and yet the scope for further development was constrained due to the mountainous terrain. Added to this were economic changes that were to lead to the end, for a considerable period, of any house-building in the Rhondda (Chapter 8). During the long period of growth the private developers had, however, made their mark. Paradoxically they were responsible for both some of the Rhondda's best housing, built for home owners with relatively high incomes, and also for most of the worst, including the notorious and insanitary cellar dwellings and many forlorn and monotonous terraces where the byelaws adopted in 1879 were barely met.

Other agencies involved in house-building, besides the colliery companies, the building clubs and speculative investors (including builders), were few. Companies not normally concerned with housing would, on occasion, venture their surplus funds in this way. The Ton Co-operative Society, for instance, submitted plans for 41 houses in 1902 and churches and chapels sometimes built, mainly in the early period on a small scale.[2]

The vast bulk of the Rhondda's housing, however, remained the domain of the colliery company, the building club and the speculative builder. Council housing came later, partly as a result of the collapse of the private housing market prior to the outbreak of the Great War. Speculative builders were responsible for most of the Rhondda's housing development in the pre-war period—their investment eclipsing that of the colliery companies and leaving the building clubs to a subsidiary, though important, role.

---

[1] Ibid.
[2] Richards, Thesis, p. 282.

Plate 1 Tyntyla Farm, Ystrad

Plate 2 Long Row, Blaenllechau

Plate 3 Glanselsig Terrace, Blaenycwm

Plate 4 Caroline Street, Blaenrhondda

Plate 5 Colliery houses at Tylorstown

Plate 6 Concrete Houses, Dinas

Plate 7 Baptist Square Blaenllechau

Plate 8 Llyn Crescent, Ferndale

Plate 9   Sherwood Street, Llwynypia

Plate 10   Fernhill Garden Suburb, Blaenrhondda

Plate 11   Eileen Place, Treherbert

Plate 12   Highfield, Maerdy

7

Water, Sanitation and Public Health

As we saw in Chapter 3, public health became a matter for legislation from the mid-nineteenth century. In the Rhondda, however, the reaction to the increasing need arising from insanitary conditions and rapid population growth was slow. The district's first medical officer of health, the 'able, many sided and fearless' Watkin Rhys, appointed in 1878, was only part-time.[1] The Rhondda was the last urban authority to make such an appointment in the whole of Glamorgan and the post was made full-time only in 1897.[2]

The continued presence of disease and ill-health in the Rhondda is not surprising given the pace of development and the reluctance of the local sanitary authority to get to grips with the issues. The newly created Glamorgan County Council, established in 1889, was concerned at the local situation and made representations to the Local Government Board to the effect that the Public Health Acts had not been properly enforced in the Rhondda and that 'other matters affecting public health required to be remedied'. In the report that followed, Dr Bruce Low, the LGB inspecting officer, concluded:

> I am of the opinion that the Local Board of Ystradyfodwg had not in the past enforced the provisions of the Public Health Acts to the extent they ought to have done ... but they are now taking large and comprehensive measures to improve the condition of their district ... Meanwhile it is not to be denied that the extremely rapid growth of this district, together with its peculiar situation in two long, deep, narrow valleys, has added greatly to the difficulties and responsibilities of the Local Authority.[3]

---

[1] GRO, Ystradyfodwg USA, 11 June 1880.
[2] RUDC, RMOH 1897; W. Williams, *A sanitary survey of Glamorganshire* (Cardiff, 1895), p. 23.
[3] Quoted in Williams, *Sanitary survey*, p. 17.

Progress, however, remained slow and in 1895 the county medical officer reported of the River Rhondda that:

> the bed and banks contain a large proportion of human excrement, stable and pig-sty manure, congealed blood, offal and entrails from the slaughter-houses, the rotten carcases of animals, cats and dogs in various stages of decomposition, old cast-off articles of clothing and bedding, old boots, old hats, bottles, tinware, ashes and street refuse, and a host of other articles ... the water is perfectly black from small coal in suspension ... the river and its tributaries form a huge open system of sewerage.[1]

Some improvement in sewage disposal was effected by the building of a number of street sewers feeding into local rivers and brooks. Construction of a main sewer from Rhondda to the coast commenced in 1885 and by 1897 nearly 15,000 (out of 19,000) homes had been linked to the main network.[2]

Water

The rivers had long been abandoned as a source of water for drinking or household use. Water was instead supplied to many streets by one of the two water companies and by some collieries, or was obtained from a variety of other sources. Much of the Rhondda Fawr (as far down as Trealaw and Penygraig) was supplied with water by the Ystrad Gas & Water Co., established in 1868, with the remaining areas supplied by the Pontypridd Water Co., established seven years later. Colliery companies in some cases supplied water to local houses, as in Llwynypia and Clydach Vale.[3]

Water from the Ystrad and Pontypridd companies was prone to pollution through poor filtration. Neither company made sufficient provision for storage, nor was able to guarantee supply during dry weather. As a result drains were unable to be flushed properly and there was a risk of water-borne diseases including typhoid fever, outbreaks of which were common.[4]

---

[1] Ibid., p. 84.

[2] RUDC, RMOH 1897. The Joint Sewerage Board (i.e. Pontypridd and Ystradyfodwg), established in 1885, started construction of the 17 mile sewer in 1889 and completed it at a cost of £156,000. Twelve miles of sewer were also built in the Rhondda Fawr and seven miles in the Rhondda Fach, linked to main sewer at Trehafod.

[3] Williams, *Sanitary survey*, p. 80. The Ystrad Gas & Water Co. also supplied gas lighting to much of the Rhondda Fawr; a similar service was provided in the Rhondda Fach by the Ferndale Gas Co. (Lewis, *Rhondda Valleys*, p. 205).

[4] Williams, *Sanitary survey*, p. 82.

By 1880 only about 4,000 Rhondda houses (44 per cent of the total) had a piped water supply and in 1885, as a consequence of the pollution affecting much of that supply, the local authority successfully took action against the Ystrad Gas & Water Co. on the grounds that they were 'unable or unwilling to provide a proper and sufficient supply of water to the district'.[1] Those without piped water also suffered from the unreliability of other sources. Problems were noted by the medical officer of health in 1883 in a number of streets, the sources of whose water is interesting in its variety.[2] These included Pit Row, Blaenllechau (which drew water from a disused coal level), Gwaunadda, Dinas (a well), Graig yr Eos, Williamstown (three wells), Baglan Street, Treherbert (a spout), Brook Street, Blaenrhondda (two spouts), seven houses near Fernhill (a duck pond), and Chicago Huts, Ynysyfeio (an old level and a stream).

While many houses had to live with an irregular supply, the local authority maintained a continuous battle with the Ystrad Gas & Water Co. The medical officer in his report of 1890 referred to 'muddy and peaty' water samples and noted that 'two putrid frogs have been drawn from the service taps, one in Gelli Road, Ton, and the other in Trealaw'. He again lamented the lack of provision for storage: 'I am informed ... that the Ystrad Gas and Water Company have to supply about 500,000 gallons daily, and still this Company have not got an ounce of storage, whereas there should be at least 30,000,000 gallons stored'. Action taken by the council against the company was, however, dismissed on account of the authority not having paid their water rate. By 1892 the position was unchanged, the medical officer reporting that 'to keep up the market value of the Ystrad Gas and Water Company's shares we, the thirsty ratepayers of Ystradyfodwg, will have to wash down our throats the summer dust with tainted water'.[3]

Privies and closets

If the water supply was poor, then the provision for effective effluent disposal was, in the early period, virtually absent. Although water closet systems were gradually installed, pails, cesspits, cesspools and ash closets predominated in the older communities. The water closets provided for the flushing of effluent via the drains to the rivers. The contents of pails and ash closets, on the other hand, were collected by 'scavengers' appointed by the

---

[1] Lewis, *Rhondda Valleys*, pp. 205, 212.
[2] Glam. Record Office, Ystradyfodwg USA, 23 Nov. 1883.
[3] Ystradyfodwg USA, RMOH 1890, 1892.

local authority and were dumped on one or other of the many scavenger tips. Such tips contained all kind of organic and non-organic refuse and were thus a major contributor to river pollution. Not surprisingly, they were considered by the county medical officer as 'par excellence most suitable media for the cultivation of germs and infectious diseases'.[1]

The need for improvements to the water supply and disposal of sewage are a constant theme in the local medical officer's reports in the 1890s. In 1898 he noted progress (in parallel with the building and connecting of sewers) in reconstructing ash closets as water closets and the retrapping and relaying of house drains. The connection of all dwellings to the Rhondda's extending sewer network, however, he acknowledged as 'impractical'.[2]

Scavenging and household refuse disposal

The medical officer also mentioned the efforts of the local authority to bring about more efficient removal of household refuse, a handbill having been distributed that read:

> Ashes and refuse must be placed in a suitable receptacle and put outside the premises every day (except Sundays) before 8 o'clock in the morning. When the receptacle has been emptied it must be at once removed from the street. All persons are warned that they are liable to a penalty if they deposit ashes or refuse upon any street, road, pavement, footway, back-lane or thoroughfare. In the case of neglect upon the part of the Scavengers, information should be sent to the District Sanitary Inspector, or the Medical Officer of Health.[3]

There were, at that time, some 19 scavenger tips, and the report called for their abolition and the establishment of a furnace for the destruction of refuse. One such tip was located opposite Oakland Terrace, Ferndale.

Death and disease

The consequence of a poor water supply and the absence, for many, of an adequate means of refuse and effluent disposal was a continuation of ill-

---

[1] Williams, *Sanitary survey*, p. 80.
[2] RUDC, RMOH 1898.
[3] Ibid.

health and disease. In 1882, a typhoid outbreak in Cymmer, though mainly confined to Argyle Street and Lincoln Street, affected 22 people over six months and resulted in four deaths. The county medical officer, in investigating the outbreak, noted that the houses had pail privies and that drains were untrapped, discharging into the stream at the lower end of Brook Street. In one house seven people in the same family were attacked by the disease.[1]

In 1899, infant mortality in the Rhondda reached its highest level at 248 per 1,000 births.[2] By this time much had been done in extending the sewer network and progress made in the provision of water closets. This enabled attention to be given to other health problems. Water for household consumption was still suspect and an outbreak of typhoid fever in Stanleytown in 1899 affected 68 people and caused ten deaths.[3] As a result of this the medical officer took further action against the Pontypridd Water Co. for their failure to fulfil an undertaking to supply water in 'a perfectly clear condition'.

Health and housing

Another issue was the problem of cellar dwellings, which were said to have fallen within the 'lowest general category'.[4] They were being built (as noted in Chapter 6) by private speculators and in 1898 and 1899 represented one in every five new dwellings in the Rhondda (with notable increases in their number in Ynyshir and Tylorstown). The county medical officer echoed local concerns, noting the presence of cellar dwellings unfit for occupation in Miskin Road (Trealaw), Ash Terrace (Pentre), Dinas Road (Dinas) and at 37–38 Co-operative Stores, Tonypandy.[5]

For housing developments generally the local authority had appointed a surveyor to ensure compliance with the newly adopted byelaws. These, however, were much flouted in the 1880s, since the authority had too few staff to monitor the continuing rapid development effectively. Gradually, conditions improved, as the byelaws adopted in 1879 were steadily revised and increasingly enforced. Other legislation available to the local authority was initially not used. The Housing of the Working Classes Act of 1890, which allowed for demolitions, the opening up of court-yards and compul-

---

[1] Williams, *Sanitary survey*, pp. 82–3.
[2] RUDC, RMOH 1899, a rate exceeded in England & Wales only by Burnley and Preston.
[3] Ibid.
[4] J. Burnett, *A social history of housing 1815–1970* (1978), p. 58.
[5] Williams, *Sanitary survey*, p. 81.

sory purchase, for which grants could be obtained from the Local Government Board, was not adopted in the Rhondda until after 1907.[1]

By 1903, the death rate in the Rhondda had reached its lowest level for 24 years, despite a typhoid outbreak in Porth that year. The medical officer's report, nevertheless, implored the council 'not to be satisfied with the present state of their District' and called for 'still greater efforts', notably in relation to water supply and refuse disposal.[2]

Improvements in water supplies

The council's patience with the Ystrad Gas & Water Co. eventually ran out and the service was municipalised in 1898, leaving the local authority and the Pontypridd Co. the main suppliers, although some communities still obtained water from private sources, notably the colliery companies:

(a) the National Colliery Co. supplied 103 houses in Blaenrhondda and 51 houses at Caroline Street from a disused level. Houses at Fernhill were similarly supplied;

(b) the Ocean Colliery Co. supplied over 500 houses in Cwmparc from surface water gathered at the foot of Graig Fawr and filtrated by the company (which owned about 200 of the houses);

(c) the Glamorgan Colliery Co. supplied nearly 300 of its own properties at Llwynypia (the 'Scotch' terraces), inadequately filtered from a gathering ground some 250 yards distant;

(d) the Cambrian Colliery Co. supplied some 800 houses in Clydach Vale, inadequately filtered from an upland gathering area and a local brook;

(e) the Ferndale Colliery Co. supplied over 200 houses at Pontygwaith and Tylorstown; and

(f) there were other private supplies of water serving dwellings at Penrhiwfer, Trebanog, Trehafod and Bush Houses, Blaenclydach.[3]

About 200 houses were still supplied from wells, springs or brooks. These included 80 at Blaenycwm (where plans were in hand to provide a supply

---

[1] W. Thompson, *Housing up-to-date* (1907), p. 38 notes that only eight Welsh authorities had adopted Part 3 of the 1890 Act.

[2] RUDC, RMOH 1903.

[3] Ibid.

WATER, SANITATION AND PUBLIC HEALTH 81

from the council's reservoir at Treherbert) and 50 at Ystrad supplied from a mountain stream.[1]

Improvements in the piped water over the following decade were substantial, with moves to provide upland reservoirs to regulate the supply and with remaining communities being provided with a municipal supply. Action was also taken against the Pontypridd Water Co. for failure to comply with statutory obligations, leading eventually to its municipalisation.[2]

Residual problems

A few communities continued to present problems in the provision of various services. In 1910 460 dwellings remained unconnected to the sewerage system, including 50 at Appletree, Dinas, which could not be easily connected because the houses lay at too low a level. At Bush Houses, Blaenclydach, the cost of sewer provision was considered too high, and the colliery company which owned the 50 houses was asked to provide pail closets instead of ash middens then in use. Over 25,000 houses now had water closets (albeit 5,000 of them being without cisterns and thus having to be flushed with buckets) and only 1,323 houses lacked separate closet accommodation.[3] The overall position was as follows:

Privies with fixed receptacles (middens, cesspits): 135
Privies with moveable receptacles: 57
Water closets (fresh water cistern flushed): 20,381
Water closets (hand, i.e. bucket flushed): 5,304

By 1916 the number of dwellings using pails, middens or cesspits had fallen to 124 and a further 4,000 houses had been fitted with cisterns, leaving just 1,000 flushed with buckets. 295 dwellings remained unconnected to the main sewerage system.[4]

Refuse disposal remained a considerable cause for concern. A Mason's Destructor was bought and erected at Ystrad in 1904 enabling fifteen of the district's 200 daily loads of refuse to be burnt. Fifteen scavenger tips, however, still remained.[5] A second destructor was erected in Dinas enabling

---

[1] Ibid., 1905, 1910.
[2] Ibid., 1906.
[3] Ibid., 1910.
[4] Ibid., 1916.
[5] Ibid., 1904.

the number of scavenger tips to be reduced to nine by 1916, although this new destructor was not used to its full capacity owing to the high cost of transporting the rubbish to it.[1]

Despite improvements in various services, housing conditions, for many, remained poor. Continuing population growth meant that overcrowding was common. In 1903 the medical officer reported 'no diminution of demand' for ordinary terraced properties for which rents of 15s to 25s per month were obtained, and noted that newly built houses were frequently occupied before being passed as fit by the district inspector.[2] One of the ironies is that, whilst overcrowding in the Rhondda was greater than in most of Glamorgan, property sizes were generally larger.[3] This reflected the high demand, the frequent taking in of lodgers and the practice of letting rooms or apartments.

The problem of cellar dwellings stubbornly remained and action taken to overcome insanitary conditions often focused, instead, on the surviving huts erected by some of the colliery companies.

Conclusion

The period up to 1914 was one in which speed of population growth and housing development outpaced, for much of the time, the provision of services. The consequences were borne by the community who had to suffer inadequate and overcrowded homes and the ill-health that went with it.

It was not until 1919 that the medical officer felt able to report that 'the District is well sewered and drained' and benefitted from an 'adequate water supply'. There was, however, still a housing shortage which, he suggested, would require the construction of 3,400 additional dwellings in the following three years. He remained reluctant to use his powers to deal with overcrowding and with cellar dwellings on account of this shortage.[4]

The houses themselves, at this time, were regarded as generally of sound construction and of a 'type suitable for the accommodation of the working classes'.[5] The main sanitary problems of the Rhondda, apart from cellar dwellings and overcrowding had, therefore, been effectively tackled.

---

[1] Ibid., 1899, 1915.
[2] Ibid., 1903.
[3] Ibid., 1910.
[4] Ibid., 1919.
[5] Ibid., 1920.

8

The Decline of the Private Sector

The urban district council, having largely dealt with the problems of water supply, sewage and refuse disposal, began to consider housing itself more carefully. To begin with, there was no thought of the council being directly involved in the building and renting of houses, although they were aware of the possibilities. From about 1900 delegates were sent to conferences on working class housing and later to others on broader issues of housing reform.[1] The council were also receiving representations locally on housing issues. In 1903 a deputation from the Rhondda Valley Workmen's Housing Committee, Blaenclydach, was heard and the council were probably urged to consider using some of the provisions of the 1890 Housing Act.[2]

By 1906 there were clear indications in many parts of South Wales that the private sector was beginning to fail.[3] Investment was going elsewhere, into co-operative societies, municipal stocks and building societies.[4] In the Rhondda, although the local authority remained content to rely on the speculative builder and the building club to meet local housing needs, they were increasingly under pressure and in 1908, in response to a letter from E.G. Culpin, secretary of the Garden City Association, it was resolved:

> that this Council affirms its belief that the present planless and haphazard extensions of towns is detrimental to the best interests of the nation, inasmuch as, by the creation of new slums and overcrowding it produces mental, moral and physical degeneration, and it is also burdensome to ratepayers; it therefore calls upon all parties to welcome the Government's promise of legislation upon the matter.[5]

---

[1] RUDC Health Committee, 25 May 1900; RUDC, 11 Aug. 1905 (at which it was agreed that delegates should attend the National Housing Reform Conference taking place at the Cheap Cottages Exhibition).

[2] RUDC, 12 June 1903. While the 1890 Act empowered local authorities to undertake demolition, rearrangement of courtyards, lending of money, compulsory purchase etc, it must be recognised that to use such provisions would have been very costly.

[3] Ministry of Health, *Report of the Regional Survey* (1920), p. 26.

[4] P. Wilding, 'Towards Exchequer subsidies for housing, 1906–1914', *Social and Economic Administration*, 6 (1972), 14.

[5] RUDC, 11 Aug. 1905. The garden city movement was at this time beginning to gain momentum and had a major impact on house design in the post-war period (see Chapter 9).

Plans were then in hand for a conference and exhibition in Swansea in 1909, organised by the National Housing Reform Council, and the council offered facilities for representatives of the Garden City Association to speak in the Rhondda. The issue of housing reform was thus firmly on the South Wales (and Rhondda) agenda.[1] Consideration of any immediate intervention on the part of the council, however, was delayed since it was clear even in 1911 that the private sector was still able to operate in the Rhondda. As the medical offer reported: 'there appears to be no abatement in the activity shown by private enterprise ... the number of new dwelling houses submitted to the Council for approval continues to maintain a high level'.[2]

First steps towards council housing

In 1912 the council, following enquiries by the Local Government Board, considered the possibility of providing houses using new powers available to them under the 1909 Housing, Town Planning Etc Act. Enquiries were made of landowners in the upper Rhondda Fach and in Penygraig, with a view to buying sites on which to build a small number of houses, so that cellar accommodation and other unfit property could be closed or cleared and the occupants rehoused.[3]

The housing crisis that was affecting much of South Wales (and other parts of the country) stemmed from a variety of factors that made it increasingly difficult to build working class houses economically, either for sale or rent. The cumulative effect of these problems was a quite sudden end to house-building immediately before the First World War. Considerable debate took place nationally as to whether the crisis was simply one of a cyclical nature (and therefore only temporary) or whether more fundamental changes were taking place in the housing market.

Building cycles

The significance of cycles in explaining fluctuations in house building has been analysed in various contexts. J.H. Richards, for instance, looked

---

[1] RUDC, 14 Feb. and 10 July 1908.

[2] RUDC Special Health Committee, 30 June 1911.

[3] RUDC, 12 Jan. 1912 (the LGB had enquired whether the council had considered taking action to provide 'small housing' at low rentals under existing legislation); Health Committee, 19 March 1912.

specifically at the relationship of building rates and the productivity of the South Wales coalfield between 1880 and 1914. For the Rhondda, he identified a cycle of some 10 to 14 years (peak to peak or trough to trough) which determined local building activity but which was different from the trend in the United Kingdom as a whole.[1] For South Wales he concluded that it seemed likely that between 1880 and 1914 the course of construction was determined by fluctuations in the export sector, which in turn was positively correlated with the building cycle in the United States. He therefore suggested that the South Wales cycle was export-determined.[2]

Various analyses of building cycles have been undertaken and it appears that, at least for a time towards the end of the nineteenth century, there was an inverse relationship between building in Britain as a whole and in the United States, although this relationship weakened as the British economy grew more complex.[3] In South Wales, however, and the Rhondda in particular, there was such a strong momentum of development as to cast doubt on the function of such building cycles locally. For example, M.J. Daunton maintains that investment in housing was essentially local, an outlet for small amounts of capital for those who wanted to keep an eye on their assets, who were not prepared to put their money into shares or send it abroad. They were not interested in small variations in the rate of interest between home and abroad or between housing and other sectors. They wanted something local and safe.[4]

The failure of the private sector

Whilst cyclical elements may form part of a broader analysis of house building, in the Rhondda it was local conditions that enabled building to be maintained over such a long period, since there was continuous high demand combined with a housing shortage up to about 1912. By the outbreak of the Great War, however, it was clear in the Rhondda, as elsewhere, that speculative investment in housing (for sale or rent) was no longer attractive. Investment was going elsewhere and some landowners were selling their

---

[1] Richards, Thesis, p. 66.

[2] J.H. Richards and J.P. Lewis, 'House building in the South Wales coalfield, 1851–1913', in W.E. Minchinton (ed.), *Industrial South Wales 1750–1914: essays in Welsh economic history* (1969), p. 242.

[3] See, e.g., essays by E.W. Cooney and H.J. Habakkuk in D.H. Aldcroft and P. Fearon (ed.), *British economic fluctuations 1790–1939* (1972). Habakkuk quotes E.H. Phelps-Brown as stating that 'whether a house is built in Oldham depends on and is decided by whether a house goes up in Oklahoma'.

[4] Daunton, *Coal Metropolis*, p. 93.

properties in order to do this.[1] The reasons for the failure of the private sector include the high price of land, the increasing price of materials, the rising cost of labour, the demand for higher standards by local authorities, the impact of the 1910 Finance Act, increases in local rates, various political factors, and the effect of lower real wages in the mining industry.

Land prices in the Rhondda had been rising as good sites became scarcer. The fact that in 1913 coal production reached a record level and miners had won a minimum wage might suggest that profits were still available to those with the resources to buy and develop land but the opportunities for such investment had diminished due to a land scarcity. Even where land had been laid out for residential development (e.g. Quarry, Mount, Canning, Gordon and Park Streets on the mountainside between Tylorstown and Ferndale) building did not start.[2] Miners' wages were, furthermore, prone to interruption through a growing number of strikes and lockouts.

Labour costs had been steadily increasing since the middle of the nineteenth century. Rates per hour for building labourers in Cardiff, for instance, had risen from 4½d per hour in 1886 to 5½d in March 1912, but then rose to 6d by July 1913 and 6½d by October 1914. Rates for tradesmen had risen in the same manner.[3] Similarly, the cost of building materials fluctuated, with peaks in 1873 and 1900, but rose steeply after 1909.[4]

The need for higher building standards arose particularly from the 1909 Town Planning Act which gave local authorities the power to make town planning schemes, defining road widths, dwelling densities, zoning of areas for different functions etc. The legislation was regarded as a considerable advance in housing policy and encouraged local authorities to undertake more inspections of unfit houses and take action to remedy defects. The Act added to the byelaw powers already in use and made more demands on house building agencies. This was especially true when the 'inflexibility' of the byelaws is considered, since these were increasingly recognised as unsuitable for hilly or mountainous areas.[5] New buildings would therefore require extra work to conform with new statutory requirements and would be more costly.

---

[1] J. Davies, 'The end of the great estates', pp. 189–93.

[2] Plans for the Duffryn Saffrwch Farm area among the Crawshay Bailey estate records mark these streets.

[3] J. Williams, *Digest of Welsh historical statistics* (Cardiff, 1985), I, p. 182.

[4] C.G. Powell, *An economic history of the British building industry 1815–1979* (1982), p. 78.

[5] *Report of the Departmental Committee on Building Byelaws, Minutes of Evidence* (Cd 9214, 1918), p. 152.

The 1910 Finance Act introduced a tax on the increase in value of development land of £1 in every £5, which had to be paid when the land was sold or the owner died. This, it was argued, made landowners reluctant to sell and led to further land shortages: 'this factor, combined with a steady increase in the cost of building materials and labour up to the time of the declaration of war brought the cost of building to a higher water-mark than it had previously reached, and the cost would have undoubtedly continued to increase even if war had not been declared'.[1]

These problems were considered by the Tudor Walters Report, which concluded that there was a

> consensus of opinion amongst the builders and land developers that the land duties ... had seriously retarded the carrying on of their business. The evidence given was that the duties had arrested the development of building estates, led to the diminution or withdrawal of financial facilities and retarded investment in house property. The taxation of builders' profits ... was considered by the builders to be an injustice, and in their opinion has seriously prejudiced the trade of house building.[2]

Mortgage lenders felt less secure and, as a consequence, some mortgages were called in.[3]

The cost of local government services formed an increasing proportion of the rents charged to tenants. Landlords were faced, therefore, with the choice of either increasing rents or accepting a lower net return on their investment. In the Rhondda landlords faced a particular dilemma because of the loss of earnings by miners involved in disputes. Most, therefore, decided to maintain rents at the same level, for which they obtained a poorer return. In 1917 W.J. Roberts noted rate increases in the period from 1901 to 1911 for 'an average cottage in South Wales of ninepence or a shilling per week'.[4]

It was suggested at the time that the existence of certain political interests, opposed to individual home ownership, was a factor in reducing investment in housing in South Wales.[5] Whilst this may be true to a small extent, it is

---

[1] Wilding, 'Towards Exchequer subsidies', p. 7.

[2] *Report of the Committee ... to consider questions of buildings construction with the provision of dwellings for the working classes* (Cd 9191, 1918), p. 7.

[3] Wilding, 'Towards Exchequer subsidies', p. 14.

[4] W.J. Roberts, 'Housing after the war', *Welsh Housing and Development Yearbook* (1917), p. 85.

[5] *Report of the Regional Survey Committee*, p. 28.

not a major consideration since there was already an exceptionally high level of home owners in the Rhondda, which seems to have been accepted, especially when achieved through such collective action as building clubs. Instead, we must look to the trade union movement as a whole and the industrial unrest that occurred in the Rhondda at this time.

Trade unionism had grown steadily and among the miners' leaders was the Rhondda MP, William Abraham ('Mabon'). There was a significant increase in strikes in the years prior to 1914. Political demands were accompanied by a revival of nonconformity in the Rhondda where trade union involvement was, for many, seen as 'a corollary of Christian faith'.[1] Disputes were the consequence, such as the Cambrian Combine lockout and strike arising out of demands for additional payments for working in 'abnormal' areas. This dispute in 1910, involving 12,000 men, led quickly to coal production in the Rhondda being brought to a standstill. The importing of blackleg labour exacerbated the situation and led to disturbances in Tonypandy and Penygraig and the despatch of troops to keep order. The strikes dragged on until the autumn of 1911, when the Cambrian men agreed to terms offered in October the previous year.[2] This prolonged dispute and the continuing political activity in the Rhondda was, it is suggested, a significant element in discouraging investment in housing. Household incomes were reduced and made it more difficult for landlords to obtain economic rents and for builders to find buyers. The national miners' stoppage in 1912 effectively destroyed any possibility of retrieving the situation or of stimulating new housing investment.

The causes of the unrest and increased political activity were, at least in part, attributed to social conditions:

> The conviction that Capital and Labour are necessarily hostile, a conviction engendered by conflict on industrial matters, has been accentuated by the fact that the social conditions of the working-classes are of an unsatisfactory character. This fact was brought out by numerous witnesses both on the employers' side and the men's side, and there can be no doubt that, although not always expressed, the workers feel deeply discontented with their housing accommodation and with their unwholesome and unattractive environment generally. The towns and villages are ugly and overcrowded, houses

---

[1] C.E. Gwyther, 'Sidelights on religion and politics in the Rhondda Valley', *Llafur*, 3 (1980), p. 34.

[2] R. Page-Arnot, *The miners: years of struggle* (1953), pp. 59–77; Egan, *Coal society*, p. 68.

are scarce and rents are increasing, and the surroundings are insanitary and depressing. The scenery is disfigured by unsightly refuse tips, the atmosphere is polluted by coal dust and smoke, and the rivers spoilt by liquid refuse from the works and factories. Facilities for education and recreation are inadequate and opportunities for the wise use of leisure are few. The influence of these social factors in the creation of industrial unrest cannot easily be measured but that their influence is great is undeniable.[1]

Such circumstances were particularly present in the Rhondda where collieries were facing a decline in productivity and greater competition—problems which could not be solved by an increase in prices.[2] The sad irony is that the resulting unrest, directed at improving conditions for miners and their families, played a major part in driving away investment needed for provision or improvement of their homes.

The reduction in real wages in the coal industry had a clear and direct effect on the willingness of miners to join or help set up building clubs, and for private developers to build for sale or rent. Real wages in the Rhondda had risen in the early 1900s to a level generally higher than in other coalfields, and this, together with the large number of families with more than one working adult and often with lodgers as well, gave households sufficient income to buy their own homes. The worsening of conditions in many pits (due to geological faults or thin seams), the effects of the 'Eight Hours Act' (restricting the hours that a miner could work), and the lack of mechanisation made it difficult for a miner to increase his income further. This, combined with a general increase in prices, reduced real wages.

Price inflation was apparent from 1902. It is difficult to assess the extent to which miners' wages kept pace in this period, but it is notable that Page-Arnot, who did not show any sympathy for the mine owners, pointed to the fact that wage demands arising around 1910 related to a desire for an 'improved standard of living' rather than to keep with inflation.[3] That their existing standard of living was jeopardised is clearly indicated by the concern over working in 'abnormal places' (where coal was difficult to extract) and price increases in the years immediately before 1914.

---

[1] 'Housing and industrial unrest', *Welsh Housing and Development Yearbook* (1918), p. 88.

[2] L.J. Williams, 'The road to Tonypandy', *Llafur*, 1 (1973), pp. 9–10.

[3] Page-Arnot, *The miners*, p. 18.

Conclusion

Various factors influenced the housing market over many years before the Great War and it was a combination of those factors that resulted in investment being lost to the Rhondda. As the Tudor Walters Report concluded in 1918: 'even before the war the financing of building schemes had become exceedingly difficult, and it was the opinion of many ... that if adequate housing schemes were to be carried out either by local authorities or private enterprise State loans would be a necessary precondition'.[1] Political upheaval and increased trade union activity were particularly important in frightening away potential investors and reducing the profitability of coal mining. Even without the effects of the Great War there would, therefore, have been a significant reduction of private house building and of activity by building clubs.

In the face of such change, the district council decided in 1912 to try to stimulate more investment in housing by using its powers under the 1899 Small Dwellings Acquisition Act.[2] A notice was issued stating that the council was prepared to consider applications for loans not exceeding £240 for leasehold property (£300 for freehold) at 4 per cent. Ownership would be vested in the council until payments were completed with the loan period not to exceed 15 years. Although the take-up of these loans was small and the council failed to stimulate the housing market, it did assist the winding up of at least one building club and may have enabled the purchase of properties by sitting tenants from landlords who wished to place their capital elsewhere. Any hope that such action might revive the private market was dashed by the Great War:

> The War has had a disastrous effect on the building industry. Owing to the shortage of labour, materials and money and their increased cost, the suspension of normal industrial activities and private housing agencies, and to various other causes, the volume of cottage building has been very greatly restricted. When the War is over, therefore, we shall be face to face with a housing problem of exceptional magnitude.[3]

A further effect was the increase in rents, a national concern that resulted in these being frozen at August 1914 levels under the 1915 Increase of Rent

---

[1] *Rep. Committee ... Dwellings for the Working Classes*, p. 7.
[2] RUDC, 1 Oct. 1912.
[3] E.L. Chappell, 'Editorial note', *Welsh Housing Yearbook* (1916), p. 17.

and Mortgage Interest (War Restrictions) Act. This was perceived by many as a temporary measure in exceptional circumstances. The difficulties following the war, however, resulted in restrictions remaining for a time, and an increasing appreciation of the need for some form of subsidised housing:

> the building clubs are falling into desuetude, and there appears to be no intention on the part of the colliery companies to undertake building operations at their own expense. There are, therefore, only two possible solutions of the difficulty, namely, extensive building by local authorities, and more liberal grants to public utility societies, in the formation of which the colliery companies could be usefully associated.[1]

After the Great War

Various committees were appointed to investigate the housing problem in the post-war period. That chaired by Lord Sumner looked at changes in the cost of living for the working classes, reporting a 7 per cent increase in costs between July 1914 and July 1918, with a disproportionate increase for the unskilled worker.[2] Tudor Walters sat on a committee chaired by James Carmichael which reported on problems in the building industry, noting the likely shortage of bricks and imported timber, and calling for the priority release from the armed forces of tradesmen and key professionals.[3] This echoed the recommendations of Walters's better known report released earlier in the year concerning dwellings for the working classes, recommending standardisation of materials and raising the possibility of state financial assistance.

Although Tudor Walters called for 'possible' state intervention, the issue had already led to heated debates in the House of Commons. In 1914 the Liberal government had pledged itself to housing reform and it is arguable that such intervention was imminent. The problems created by the Great War simply provided the final and considerable precipitating factor.[4] To combat the post-war housing crisis the government established a scheme to give

---

[1] Jevons, *Coal trade*, p. 129.

[2] *Report of the Committee appointed to enquire into and report upon ... the cost of living to the working classes ... which may have arisen under war conditions* (Cd 8980, 1918), p. 7.

[3] *Report of the Committee appointed ... to consider the position of the building industry after the war* (Cd 9197, 1918), p. 6.

[4] Wilding, 'Towards Exchequer subsidies', pp. 13–16.

financial help to private developers and local authorities enabling them to build and manage dwellings. Money was to be available from the Public Works Loan Board at 5½ per cent although some local authorities were required to seek loans from private sources.[1] Because the income from rents would fall short of expenditure the Local Government Board was prepared to subsidise approved schemes. The optimism of those who wished to build such housing schemes was, however, short-lived. The 1919 Housing Act, whilst ambitious and relatively generous in its subsidies, only managed to produce 170,000 houses in the public sector and a further 39,000 private dwellings, whereas 500,000 had been promised.[2]

In the Rhondda the council shared the difficulties faced by other authorities and, as described in the next chapter, failed to use the legislation to the extent they would have wished or, indeed, that was needed to combat local problems. Ironically the President of the Local Government Board which was responsible for restricting the council's earliest proposals was Lord Rhondda, i.e. D.A. Thomas, formerly head of the Cambrian Combine.

[1] 'The government's housing scheme', *Welsh Housing and Development Yearbook* (1919), p. 87.

[2] M.J. Daunton (ed.), *Councillors and tenants: local authority housing in English cities 1919–1939* (Leicester, 1984), p. 9.

9

Housing Reform and the Emergence of Council Housing

By the end of the First World War, housing policy was becoming concerned not just with overcoming shortages but also, through subsidies, with the provision of a quality of housing that had previously been out of reach of the working classes. The types of housing proposed had little in common with byelaw housing (typically terraces) but instead following the model set by the garden cities. This was true of both the public and private sectors. Already the 1909 Town Planning Act had given local authorities power to control developments—their numbers, height, density and so on—together with road layouts, widths and open space provision.[1]

Garden cities and new ideas

The garden city movement was first given expression in the development of Letchworth Garden Suburb (Herts.), begun in 1903. The key features emerged from the ideas of Ebenezer Howard who maintained that houses should, as far as possible, be well spaced out, e.g. in culs de sac, with gardens and side access, each dwelling having a coal store, closet and larder. A definition of 'garden city' adopted in 1919 by the Garden Cities and Town Planning Association in consultation with Ebenezer Howard was 'a town designed for healthy living and industry; of a size that makes possible a full measure of social life, but not larger; surrounded by a rural belt; but the whole of the land being in public ownership or held in trust for the community'. Before the Great War more than 50 schemes on garden city lines had been started in Britain and some 11,000 houses built. Their success and popularity led to their being accepted as the main model for council housing. Delegates from Rhondda UDC attended various conferences, lectures and exhibitions, including one at Letchworth in 1905.[2] Public

---

[1] J.A. Lovat-Fraser, 'What town planning means', *Welsh Housing Yearbook* (1916), p. 37.
[2] RUDC, 11 Aug. 1905.

awareness was further increased by articles in the *Western Mail* and *South Wales Daily News* in 1911.[1] What had not been resolved was how garden city ideas could be developed without some form of subsidy to ensure that rents were kept at affordable levels.[2]

Various bodies were established to promote garden city ideas and housing developments. In Wales these included the Housing Reform Co. (1911) and various public utility societies such as the Welsh Town Planning and Housing Trust Ltd (1913), Welsh Garden Cities Ltd (*c.* 1914) and the South Wales Garden Cities and Town Planning Association, which merged with the Welsh Housing Association to form the Welsh Housing and Development Association of 1917. The Housing Reform Co. was established by H.S. Jevons who had a strong interest in planning and social reform. He resigned as Professor of Economics at University College, Cardiff, to become managing director. The company had three main objectives: to create co-operative societies in order for them to own houses built by the company; to promote the adoption of town planning principles; and to introduce new techniques leading to improved house planning and construction.[3] Jevons was committed to garden city designs and by May 1912 four schemes were planned: Rhiwbina near Cardiff, Caerphilly, Merthyr Tydfil and, close to the Rhondda, Ynysybwl. The scheme at Rhiwbina was started first, although it soon got into difficulty. Unable to borrow sufficient money, the sponsoring company went into liquidation in 1914.[4] Jevons departed for India and the *Cardiff Times* reported that:

> the idealist had lost both his own private fortune and that of his wife in his effort to provide decent homes for the working classes. He had no resources on which to draw. To continue his work would be hopeless. He had attempted to build bricks without straw and he had discovered it was beyond his powers.[5]

Public utility societies, given extended borrowing powers under the 1909 Town Planning Act, were advocated as a 'third arm' for house-building. Some twenty societies were set up in Wales which by 1916 had planned or

---

[1] Daunton, *Coal metropolis*, p. 101.

[2] M. Swenarton, *Homes fit for heroes: the politics and architecture of early state housing* (1981), p. 24.

[3] A.K. Hignell, 'Suburban development in north Cardiff 1850–1919: a case-study of the patterns and processes of growth in the parishes of Llanishen, Lisvane and Whitchurch' (University of Wales [Cardiff] Ph.D. thesis, 1987), p. 371.

[4] Ibid., p. 386.

[5] Quoted, ibid.

built 2,200 houses. One such society, established by the local colliery company, was at Fernhill, Treherbert, which built 14 houses for sale and rent (Plate 10). Their original intention had been to build 599 dwellings but, like other societies, their aspirations were thwarted through an inability to borrow enough money, even though a government loan for £29,866 was approved.[1] Other organisations had wider interests. The Welsh Town Planning and Housing Trust, for instance, set up housing societies to build garden villages and estates under its supervision.[2] Described by Jevons as a 'semi-philanthropic company' offering a dividend to investors of up to 5 per cent, it was established by David Davies (by then an MP) of the Ocean Colliery Co. and was responsible for schemes at Barry, Wrexham, Machynlleth and Llanidloes. It also helped to carry on the scheme at Rhiwbina after the demise of the Housing Reform Co. Other schemes were developed at Ely (Cardiff) and, closer to the Rhondda, at Llantrisant.[3]

Welsh Garden Cities Ltd operated on a similar basis, often in collaboration with colliery companies, and by 1916 their projects included Hendreforgan (Gilfach Goch), just outside the Rhondda, which was planned to have some 400 dwellings by the 1920s. Their developments, however, although bearing the garden city label, fell far short of the ideals put forward by Ebenezer Howard. As E.G. Culpin observed: 'in a large proportion of them the term is a misnomer and in some instances the very things which the Garden City movement hoped to cure are being perpetuated. In the matter of layout, the architecture, the construction, the standard falls deplorably.'[4] The Welsh Housing and Development Association was simply an educational and advisory body which published widely on housing matters and helped to increase awareness of many issues. In 1917, it had over 50 affiliated trade unions and many members who were active in other housing organisations.[5]

---

[1] 'Public utility societies in Wales', *Welsh Housing Yearbook* (1916), p. 60.

[2] As noted by T. Alwyn Lloyd in the *Report of the Departmental Committee on Building Byelaws, Minutes of Evidence* (Cd 9214, 1918), p. 149.

[3] Jevons, *Coal trade*, p. 653; Hignell, Thesis, p. 387; 'Public utility societies', p. 58.

[4] E.G. Culpin, 'What a garden city is', *Welsh Housing Yearbook* (1916), p. 66.

[5] As noted by Chappell, Jenkins and Ruthen (*Report of the Departmental Committee on Building Byelaws, Minutes of Evidence*, p. 166).

Council housing: a beginning

The problems facing any agency wishing to build houses on garden city lines in the Valleys were considerable. In the Rhondda it was claimed in 1919 that 3,400 additional houses were needed but, because of the steep hillsides, low density development was extremely difficult.[1] Rhondda UDC had been looking for sites since 1912 and by 1919 had resolved to buy land and build houses at Penygraig. They were also drawing up plans for a scheme at Maerdy.[2] Progress, however, was slow. The Local Government Board (which gave permission for such schemes) delayed agreeing the necessary borrowing despite an earlier circular stating the government's recognition of the need for 'substantial' financial assistance from public funds in areas of housing need where local authorities were prepared to build houses. Authorisation was eventually given, later in 1919, to seek tenders for both the Penygraig and the Maerdy schemes.[3] The council initially favoured the former but the tenders returned were too high and costs were only reduced by design changes which removed a number of retaining walls, excluded fireplaces for sculleries etc.[4]

A meeting in spring 1920 with the local master builders' federation heard expressions of willingness by contractors to work for the council, but highlighted the shortage of skilled labour, lack of materials and fluctuating prices.[5] The council's estimates indicated an average cost of £1,147 for the proposed houses at Penygraig including carriageways, sewers, footways etc, but excluding loan charges and incidental expenses.[6] Three basic types of house were planned, the smallest being three-bedroomed, non-parlour houses, while the largest had four bedrooms and a parlour. The start of construction on this site, however, was still over a year away.

With the council committed to building houses, the first development could not wait for the difficulties at Penygraig to be resolved. Major subsidence at Edward Street, Maerdy, meant that many families were living in houses in a 'very dilapidated and dangerous condition'. The council responded by putting up fifteen war surplus huts in Maerdy Park.[7] These were made from corrugated iron lined with matchboarding with a brick

---

[1] RUDC, RMOH 1919.
[2] RUDC, 11 July 1913; Health Committee, 25 June 1918.
[3] RUDC, 25 Sept. 1917, 26 April and 16 June 1919.
[4] RUDC Housing Committee, 21 Oct. 1919.
[5] Ibid., 27 Jan. 1920; RMOH 1919.
[6] RUDC Housing Committee, 23 Dec. 1919.
[7] Ibud., 27 May 1920.

fireplace and chimney. They cost £400 each and were offered for rent at 7s 3d per week (or 8s 3d for some larger types). They were, however, inadequate in cold weather and, though properly drained, were not connected to the main sewer network.[1] The 1919 Housing Act also allowed local authorities to give support to private contractors to build houses which would then be bought by councils for rent. In the Rhondda, the council supported developments by private builders at Taff Street and Eileen Place, Treherbert, and at Llanfair Road and Mikado Street, Penygraig.[2]

At last, on 22 June 1920, after lengthy negotiations with the Ministry of Health and the Pontypridd and Rhondda Valleys Master Builders' Association, contracts were sealed to build 44 houses in Penygraig at Bransby Street, Millbourne Street and Aubrey Road, a reduction from an original proposal for 160 dwellings. The development would use three contractors, J. Thomas (who built 1–6 and 31–38 Millbourne Street), W. Pugh (7–12 Millbourne Street and 1–8 Bransby Street), and F.G. Rideout (1–6 Aubrey Road and 35–44 Bransby Street), and would be at an overall price of £90,171.[3] By the autumn of 1921 the first houses at Penygraig and, by the end of 1921, some privately built council houses at Eileen Place, Treherbert (Plate 11), had been completed and the tenants had moved in (Appendix 3).

The Ministry of Health demanded that rents should be higher than proposed by the council, and these were finally set at between 7s 6d and 11s for Penygraig and 8s to 10s for the privately built houses. The council, however, managed to obtain the agreement of the ministry to a lower rent (due to the diminishing earnings of local miners) than would otherwise have been charged.[4] An example of the smaller non-parlour type of house (though generous in size by later standards) is 37 Bransby Street (Fig. 9.1), which had three sizeable bedrooms, a bathroom and coal store, larder etc. The estate was built to a relatively low density and the houses were semi-detached with sizeable gardens and side access. The houses were let to tenants ('each application on its merits') by the council's Housing Committee.[5] The design of the houses and their layout owed much to garden city ideas that had rapidly gained favour in Wales as a reaction to the deprivations of living in substandard and overcrowded terraced housing.

---

[1] RUDC Housing Committee, 22 June 1920; RMOH 1920 and 1921.

[2] RUDC, 14 April 1920.

[3] RUDC Housing Committee, 22 June 1920. The price was significantly greater than the council's original estimate.

[4] RUDC Housing Committee, 21 March 1922.

[5] Ibid., 12 Jan. 1922.

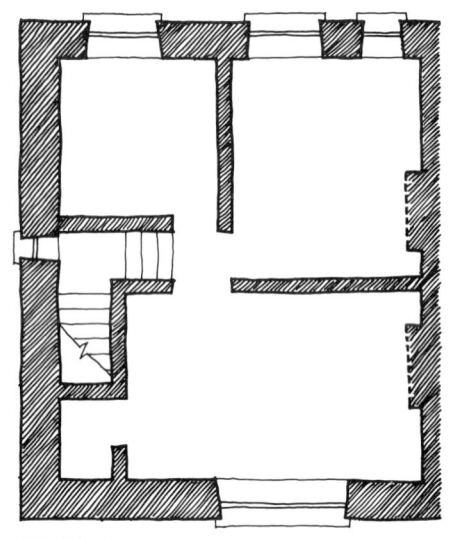

FIRST FLOOR.

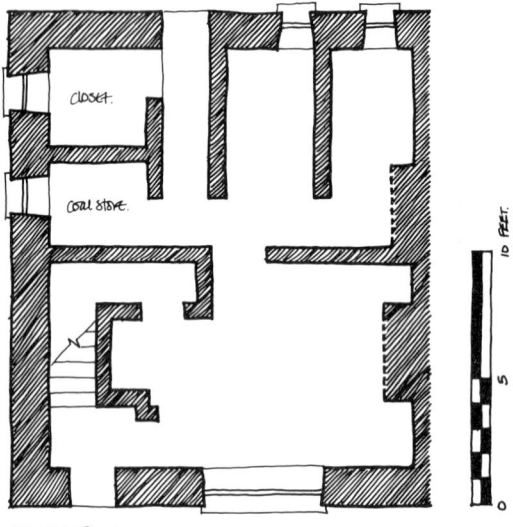

GROUND FLOOR.

9.1 37 Bransby Street, Penygraig

Byelaw issues

While considerable debate by the Welsh Town Planning and Housing Trust was taking place concerning the building of houses, there was a continuing discussion of the byelaws, particularly after the publication of the Tudor Walters Report. Problems with byelaw housing had been apparent in the Valleys for a long time, and yet local authorities followed slavishly, almost without exception, the models put forward by the Local Government Board, despite their unsuitability for hilly terrain. As C.F. Ward argued:

> Is it not absurd to have the same laws governing the construction of roads and houses on a hill-side as on a flat piece of land? What does this really mean? First, as to the width of the road; it is necessary in order to conform with these by-laws to construct hill-side roads at least 36ft wide. This means cutting into the hill on one side of the road and filling up on the other. When we erect houses more excavation is required on the upper side, producing a dwelling with the windows looking on to a bank and thus spoiling the garden view while the house on the lower side opposite has to have a basement without through ventilation and an additional flight of steps to gain access to the garden. The latter house is very costly to build, and as a result the rent has to be fixed at a price quite above its value considering the accommodation and conveniences.[1]

He suggested more liberal byelaws, with provision for narrower street widths, simpler drainage patterns and lower ceiling heights.

While the indications are of considerable local government apathy on this issue, some Valleys authorities (e.g. Abersychan and Abertillery urban districts and Pontardawe RDC) did amend their byelaws. Others, such as Rhondda, which held to byelaws more suited to lowland areas, were, it has been argued, effectively pushing up house-building costs by between £20 and £50 per dwelling.[2] A departmental report (overlapping to some extent with the Tudor Walters Report) called for local authorities to be permitted greater flexibility as well as affording them stronger powers to combat byelaw evasion.[3] Such recommendations were perhaps an inevitable response given

---

[1] C.F. Ward, 'Town plannning in the Welsh valleys', *Welsh Housing Yearbook* (1916), p. 85.

[2] *Report of the departmental committee on building byelaws* (Cd 9213, 1918), pp. 180, 172.

[3] Ibid., p. 16.

the depth of feeling obvious from the reports presented by the Welsh Housing and Development Association and the Welsh Town Planning and Housing Trust. These expressed the view that the existing byelaws led to 'the most appalling forms of building' and suggested an alternative approach allowing for 'narrower roads following the contour of the ground, with houses built on the upper side only'. The call for local authorities to adopt (and enforce) more flexible byelaws was echoed in evidence submitted by the WHDA, which noted the 'apathy and ineptitude' of local government in the region. They asked the Local Government Board

> to draft a code of byelaws particularly applicable to South Wales ... a special code of street bye laws ... for the purpose of submitting to officials and members of local authorities in South Wales in order that they may have some model and some incentive before them to remodel their codes.[1]

Continued rigid implementation of byelaws was blamed as being 'practically responsible for the origin of cellar dwellings and the worst forms of overcrowding'.[2] 'Model' designs which began to be devised for hillside locations therefore offered wide frontages and limited depth.

Council housing: reductions in standards

While the earliest council housing in the Rhondda, at Penygraig, embraced many ideas of the garden city movement, subsequent developments had to compromise. This, it appears, would not have unduly worried the Local Government Board whose 'unadventurous outlook' was 'torn between late Victorian stereotypes and the emerging pattern of suburban estates'.[3]

The Penygraig scheme was developed on gently sloping land and did not have to confront the difficulties presented by steeper sites. The subsequent development of 50 houses at Maerdy (Highfield), however, built under the 1923 Housing Act (with a lower level of subsidy), had a higher density. The houses were smaller than those at Penygraig and were built in terraces. They offered reasonable sized gardens and 30 dwellings included a parlour as well as the standard living room, scullery, bathroom and three bedrooms (Plate

---

[1] Ibid., pp. 152, 167–8.

[2] C.T. Ruthen, 'The town planning movement in Wales', *Welsh Housing and Development Yearbook* (1917), p. 72.

[3] C.G. Powell, 'Fifty years of progress', *Built Environment* (Oct. 1974), p. 352.

12). The lowering of standards reflected a shift in government policy which gave less support for council housing. The best of those built in the Rhondda are, as a consequence, the early scheme in Penygraig. The first houses at Maerdy were completed at the end of 1924 (Appendix 3).

Houses with the same design as Maerdy (both parlour and non-parlour types) were built at Wattstown in 1926. There were, however, substantial delays, with the council deducting £129 from payments due to the contractor on account of 'particular circumstances' that led to the delays, and in the end having to complete the work themselves.[1] The houses at Wattstown, due to the mountainside location, in some cases had restricted gardens (either lacking a front garden or having cramped back yards). The internal layout of the parlour houses is illustrated by 85 Pleasant View (Fig. 9.2). Whilst space standards were still relatively generous compared with older housing, the impact of more limited subsidies can be seen, notably by the reversion to long terraces which, although in keeping with local tradition, ignored garden city ideals. Such ideals had some impact on the Rhondda's council housing, notably in the first scheme at Penygraig. Set against the district's housing needs, however, the council's efforts made only a minimal contribution.

Problems in the private sector

The private sector had stopped building houses in the Rhondda except in the smallest numbers. In 1924 there was an estimated need for 5,066 dwellings but only 165 houses had been built in the previous three years, over 100 of which had been erected by (or for) the district council.[2] The extent of housing need was calculated as follows:

Houses required to relieve overcrowding in 1921	3,232
Houses required for natural increase in population	1,430
Houses required to replace unfit tenements	569
Total	5,231
Less houses built since 1921	165
Total number of houses needed	5,066

---

[1] RUDC Housing Committee, 27 July 1926.
[2] RUDC, RMOH 1924.

102 THE EMERGENCE OF COUNCIL HOUSING

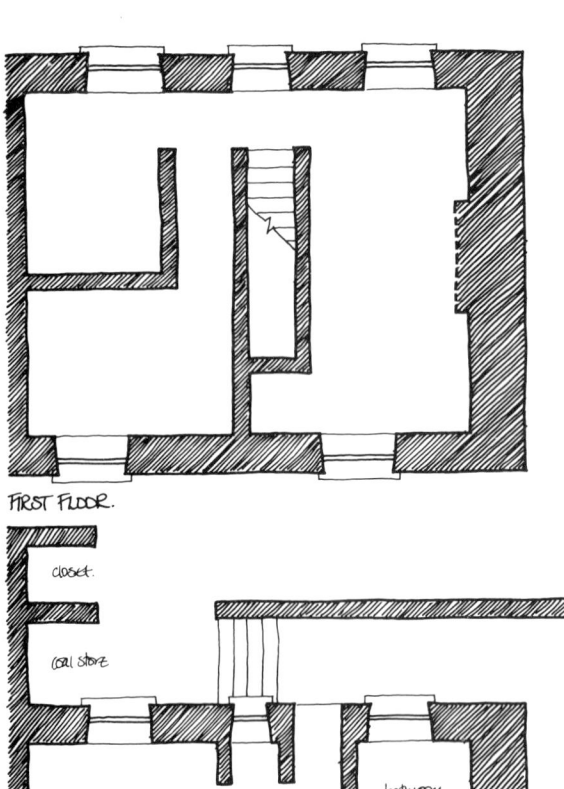

FIRST FLOOR.

closet.
coal store.

bathroom.

GROUND FLOOR.

0   5   10 FEET.

9.2 85 Pleasant View, Wattstown

This lack of progress was in spite of the falling price of materials. The schedules adopted by the Pontypridd and Rhondda Valleys Master Builders' Association show significant reductions between December 1920 and June 1923, notably for timber, including laths (58 per cent, although these had begun to increase again in later 1923), and for drainage and rainwater goods (56 per cent). Smaller reductions were evident for ironmongery (29 per cent), slates (31 per cent) and bricks, plaster etc (40 per cent).[1] These falls, however, were short-lived and, in any case, prices never fell to pre-war levels. As E.L. Chappell pointed out in 1923:

> At the present time the average cost of building in South Wales is approximately 110% above that of 1914 ... The drop in prices has not been considerable and in the case of some classes of material, e.g. timber, the trend has been upwards ... present circumstances do not point to any further big reductions during the current year.[2]

Reductions in material costs were, in any case, not matched by a fall in the cost of labour. Furthermore the political and economic situation remained uncertain, with continuing strife between the miners and their employers and a shrinking export market for coal. Many miners and their families had remained in debt following disputes in 1921, which led to reductions in wages and manpower. In the words of Page-Arnot, 'The effect of the National Wages Agreement of July 1921 was that coal-mining, from being for a short time one of the best paid trades, fell to being one of the worst paid'.[3] While the Rhondda represented an extreme, the same problems were evident elsewhere and it was clear that no revival of the private sector was likely, at least in the near future. Many builders had to survive on repair and improvement work or diversify. A number became undertakers, using their carpenters for coffin making and their horses and carts for funerals.[4]

The Welsh Housing and Development Association were aware of the problem and issued a special manifesto for the 1923 election campaign, which stated that there was

---

[1] Pontypridd and Rhondda Valleys Masters Builders' Federation, 'Schedule of prices, building materials and labour' (unpublished booklet); I indebted to Morley and Clarence Fox of Ferndale, respectively a retired mason and carpenter, for this reference.

[2] E.L. Chappell, 'The case for municipal housing', *Welsh Housing and Development Yearbook* (1923), p. 45.

[3] Page-Arnot, *The miners*, p. 339.

[4] Information from Morley and Clarence Fox.

no immediate prospect of houses being built to let at commercial rents, that for some time to come it would be necessary to rely largely on the activities of municipal bodies and other agencies, and that deficits were bound to occur in all working-class housing schemes, to meet which contributions would be required from State funds ... no private speculator is, therefore, likely to embark on cottage building enterprises to let to tenants.[1]

The district council, frustrated by the lack of progress, held a special meeting in July 1923 to discuss the problems. They agreed to offer a subsidy of £100 per house, 'subject to satisfactory safeguards', to encourage building by local enterprises. By November 1925, however, only 66 such grants had been made.[2] It was agreed, furthermore, that the clerk should meet the chairman of the Committee of Representatives of Colliery Proprietors 'with a view to ascertaining whether the colliery companies would be prepared to assist in the erection of houses'. This resulted in just twelve houses being built by Glenavon Garw Collieries at Blaenycwm.[3]

By 1928, the council had made a further 305 loans under the 1899 and 1919 Small Dwellings Acquisition Acts, amount to £68,375, mostly in the post-war period. Such advances, however, did nothing to increase the size of the overall housing stock, but simply enabled sitting tenants to purchase houses from their landlords (or, as in the pre-war period, from a building club).[4] The attempts to encourage public utility societies (as promoted by the Welsh Town Planning and Housing Trust), as successors to the building clubs (but where the members had limited liability) were similarly unsuccessful. The only one in the Rhondda was that at Fernhill, Treherbert.

Deterioration of the older housing

The initiatives taken by the council and others had no real impact on Rhondda's housing shortage and proposals to demolish unfit properties or close cellar dwellings were repeatedly postponed.[5] The problems were made

---

[1] Chappell, 'Municipal housing', p. 43.

[2] RUDC, 31 July 1923, 10 Nov. 1926.

[3] RUDC Housing Committee, 8 Aug. 1923; 27 May 1924. It appears that a small number of additional dwellings may also have been built at Blaenycwm by the colliery company.

[4] E.A Charles, 'Activities of local authorities in Wales and Monmouthshire', *Welsh Housing and Development Yearbook* (1928), p. 97.

[5] This is clear from meetings over many years of the RUDC Health Committee.

worse by subsidence. The extent of this varied but a local re-levelling exercise by the Ordnance Survey between 1898 and 1910 revealed that many places had sunk by between five and eight feet.[1]

At Oakland Terrace, Ferndale, in 1922, extensive repairs were required following subsidence, responsibility for which was accepted (following pressure from the council and probably the ground landlords, the Crawshay Bailey estate) by the colliery company (by then part of the Cambrian combine).[2] The council assisted the improvements by erecting a small single-storey dwelling as temporary accommodation while the works were in progress, ownership then being transferred to the colliery company. While some dwellings (as at Oakland Terrace) required major works, others suffered from damp penetration, damage to plasterwork, joinery etc. The loss of jobs in the pits meant, in addition, less concessionary coal and fewer fires in the hearth to keep dampness at bay.

Poverty and depression

With the depressed state of the Rhondda's economy inward migration stopped. There was, nevertheless, still a need in 1926 for over 4,500 dwellings. The urban district council's contribution of 172 dwellings (by the end of that year) with a further 66 in 1927, was thus paltry.[3] Conditions for everyone were worsening, with many tenants and owners unable to pay their rent or mortgage. Early in 1928 the council considered 38 cases of rent arrears (22 of which were at Highfield, Ferndale), and were having difficulty finding tenants who could afford to rent some of the larger houses at Penygraig. By 1930 there was an additional problem of absconding tenants.[4] Private landlords, at the same time, were more reluctant to undertake repairs and to put right 'nuisances' drawn to their attention by the council.[5]

1926 represented the lowest point in the history of industrial relations in the Rhondda, with the coalowners again seeking to reduce wages, which led to the General Strike, followed by a protracted national miners' dispute. When the men returned to work the struggle in South Wales had lasted over seven months and wages earned by miners (which in 1925–6 were already

---

[1] Jevons, *Coal trade*, p. 197.
[2] Information from Morley and Clarence Fox; see also RUDC, RMOH 1922.
[3] RUDC, RMOH 1925; Charles, 'Activities', p. 96.
[4] RUDC Sub-Committee on Arrears, 13 Jan. 1928; Housing Committee, 1 Jan. 1929, 27 May 1930.
[5] RUDC, RMOH 1926.

well below the levels of 1920–1) continued to fall.[1] Many pits closed or reduced their workforce. No area was as badly affected as the Rhondda, where just three out of four miners who went on strike were able to return to work.[2] The scale of poverty was considerable. In the Pontypridd Poor Law Union (which included the Rhondda) 94,000 people received relief out of a population of 315,000.[3] The amount of relief was reduced by the implementation of restrictive scales for locked-out miners, imposed by the Ministry of Health, and by the fact that the Pontypridd Board of Guardians relied for part of their income from tonnages of coal sold.[4] Of Maerdy it was said that the village 'was so depressed, so poverty stricken, that people suffered from malnutrition. Some people committed suicide, some people were taken into the mental home'.[5] In such a situation the need was simply to survive. Mortgage and rent payments might, understandably, have taken second place to food and warmth. Subletting inevitably increased as did the extent of overcrowding and the number of vacant dwellings.[6] No private developer would consider building for rent or sale in this situation and it is not surprising that such building in the Rhondda was virtually non-existent.

The council was unable to overcome the problem. Given the local situation the suggestion by the Ministry of Health early in 1927 that the private sector should be encouraged was unrealistic, even though the motive was in part a reluctance 'to sanction ... further loans which would have the effect of throwing additional burdens on the local rates'.[7] The government, at this time, was increasingly concerned about local authority spending. S.V. Ward has pointed out that:

> Overall we can conclude that the prime intention of local authority capital spending in the inter-war period was to reinforce spontaneous private investment ... in particular there was a marked reluctance to sanction public capital spending in areas with poor prospects.[8]

---

[1] Page-Arnot, *The miners*, p. 527.

[2] P. Jeremy, 'Life on Circular 703: the crisis of destitution in the South Wales coalfield during the lockout of 1926', *Llafur*, 2 (1977), p. 73.

[3] Ibid., p. 68.

[4] Ibid. Pontypridd Guardians, having borrowed to pay relief, were nearly half a million pounds in debt by the end of 1926.

[5] '1926 remembered and revealed', *Llafur*, 2 (1977), p. 25. W. Picton is quoted in this article.

[6] RUDC, RMOH 1928.

[7] RUDC Housing Committee 22 Feb. 1927.

[8] S.V. Ward, 'Interwar Britain: a study of government spending, planning and uneven economic development', *Built Environment*, 17 (1981), p. 102.

The Rhondda was clearly such an area and the council was undoubtedly considered a 'high risk' authority, meeting none of the criteria set by the Ministry of Health for assessing loan applications.[1]

Ironically, the problems of housing need arising from overcrowding were partially overcome by the poverty of the area, which drove thousands away in search of work elsewhere. The proportion of houses occupied by more than one family fell from 33 per cent in 1923–4 to 26 per cent in 1930, and the average number of persons per house from 6.0 to 5.1. By 1930 the medical officer had dramatically changed the emphasis of his reports, remarking that 'the district is practically free from slum areas and the only highly unsatisfactory class of occupied property ... consists of separately occupied basement tenements which aggregate over 460 in number'.[2]

Dealing with the cellar dwellings

The medical officer of health advocated swift action to deal with cellar dwellings, a problem which had been acknowledged for three decades but survived on account of the lack of other housing. By 1933 the council had resolved to undertake small housing schemes at King Street, Gelli, and Mountain View, William Street and Church Street, Trealaw, to rehouse the occupants of cellars in those communities.[3] These were the last houses to be built by the council before the Second World War, by which time they had just 287 permanent council houses.[4] The King Street properties were completed in July 1936; those in Trealaw, to the same design, some nine months later.[5] The Trealaw scheme was for 27 dwellings, mostly with three bedrooms, and was built by the lowest tenderer, Benjamin Roberts of Trealaw.[6] Standards were significantly lower than in previous schemes and all the houses lacked parlours. A typical example is 20 Church Street (Fig. 9.3) which comprises three bedrooms, a living room, bathroom and scullery. The closet and coal store are in the back yard.

---

[1] Ibid., p. 101. The criteria for high risk authorities were: high rates, falls in rateable value, sharp increases in poor relief spending, heavy indebtedness in relation to rateable value, rating arrears, unexercised borrowing powers, poor economic prospects, and financial irregularities. Many depressed areas would fall foul of most of these.

[2] RUDC, RMOH 1930.

[3] RUDC Housing Committee, 27 Feb. 1934.

[4] Rhondda Borough Council, *Rhondda District Plan. Report. 1. Population.*

[5] RUDC Housing Committee, 23 June 1936, 23 March 1937; cf. Appendix 3.

[6] Ibid., 26 Nov. 1935.

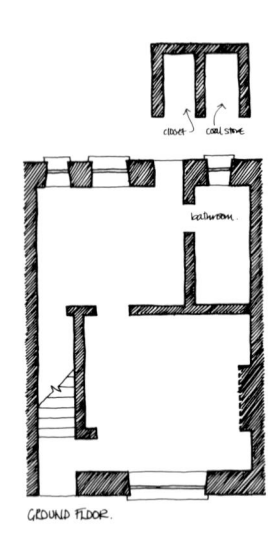

9.3 20 Church View, Llwynypia

The later 1930s

In 1933 the council held a meeting with local builders to discuss the need for more housing and was told that 'the erection for houses by private enterprise ... could not be regarded as adequately remunerative in view of the uncertain conditions prevailing in the coalmining industry and the consequent inability of the prospective tenants to pay an economic rent'.[1] Loans were, in any case, almost impossible to obtain for house-building in the Rhondda. The council's surveyor, for instance, meeting the managing director of the Principality Building Society in Cardiff to inquire about money to assist Rhondda's private builders, was informed that 'the Society were not prepared to entertain the suggestion'.[2]

Given the impossibility of reviving the private sector, the council could only forge ahead with developments of its own. Housing need had continued to drop on account of outmigration and so a mere 400 more dwellings were considered necessary at the end of 1936.[3] In just four months of that year 287 families had been helped to move to other areas and thus there was a consequent reduction in overcrowding.[4] By 1938, known overcrowding had fallen to 249 dwellings, of which 130 were cases of living 'in apartments'.[5] Schemes were planned in 1939 for 20 more houses at Penygraig (extending the development at Bransby Street and Millbourne Street) and a further 20 at Blaenycwm. The new Penygraig scheme was, in face, due to start but was cancelled at the outbreak of war.[6]

Broader public health issues

Although council house-building between the wars was slow, progress was made with other public health problems. Few scavenger tips remained by 1937 and two-thirds of household refuse was being incinerated at the Dinas destructor. Drainage and sewerage facilities, though often disrupted by breakages due to subsidence, were systematically improved with links made to isolated streets (including Appletree, Dinas, in 1922 and Bush Houses, Blaenclydach, in 1932), leaving only 100 dwellings unconnected. Just 86

---

[1] RUDC, RMOH 1933; Housing Committee 26 Sept. 1933.
[2] RUDC Housing Committee, 27 Feb. 1934.
[3] Ibid., 22 Dec. 1936.
[4] RUDC, RMOH 1936.
[5] RUDC, RMOH 1938.
[6] RUDC Housing Committee, 21 Feb., 25 July, 21 Nov. 1939.

privies with fixed or moveable receptacles (middens, cesspits or pails) remained and only 2,300 water closets were flushed with buckets.[1] Water supplies had been extended to many dwellings formerly served by colliery companies, notably the new services provided to Clydach Vale (1926–30), Caroline Street and Fernhill, Blaenrhondda (1931 and 1934), Bush Houses, Blaenclydach (1932), and Llewellyn Street and Brewery Street, Pontygwaith (1938). This left Cwmparc as the one major area supplied privately (by the Ocean Coal Co.).[2] More specifically, and particularly after 1930 (thanks to outmigration and the development of new council housing schemes), the authority was able to take action in closing and demolishing unfit properties, issuing abatement notices and encouraging owners to put right nuisances, where necessary undertaking work in default of the owner.[3]

Poverty, however, persisted. A survey of Tonypandy, Trealaw and Penygraig in 1936 found 'quite a large proportion of the households were below the poverty line, and therefore living under conditions in which no human being should be forced to live'.[4] As a contemporary observed:

> the cost of unemployment must not only be reckoned objectively in terms of the cost of social services and the loss of production, but also subjectively in terms of the waste of human material and its effect on standards of living, health and general morale.[5]

Conclusion

Although throughout the inter-war period the Rhondda was characterised by rapid decline, terrible poverty and stagnation in house-building, there were some positive changes. The council, in making its first ventures into housing and later in taking stronger action on other public health issues, contributed significantly to improvements in living conditions. Their tenacity was particularly apparent in the early years when the cost of developments and the obstructiveness of the Ministry of Health conspired to stop or delay so

---

[1] RUDC, RMOH 1937.

[2] RMOH, various years.

[3] Ibid.

[4] RUDC, RMOH 1937. Of the 1,769 dwellings surveyed, there were over a hundred instances of repairs to walls, roofs, doors, floors etc of WCs (320); flushing appliances (177); external works to house (832); internal works (617); unblocking of WCs (115); unblocking of drains (105); paving of yard or other areas (204); and wall or fence repair or renewal (184).

[5] J.R.E. Phillips, 'Sources of income in a distressed area of South Wales', *Welsh Housing and Development Yearbook* (1936), p. 53.

many of their proposals. It was, however, the Rhondda's economic decline and the inadequacy of government subsidies that limited the contribution of council housing in the area during this period.

Making the problem worse from the private developer's point of view was the cost of rates, a burden that was particularly great in areas of decline. As Mr and Mrs Hicks, in examining rate burdens in 1937–8, pointed out: 'to a very large extent high rates are due to poverty ... declining areas tend to have high rates, and the high rates hasten the decline'. They argued that since high rates tended to deter the development of new housing 'it is economically right that this drawback should be offset by housing subsidies' and higher subsidies should be available in more highly rated areas.[1]

As we have seen, the private sector in the Rhondda offered no solution to the problems faced by the two valleys. Barely a hundred private houses were built in the inter-war period. Only after the Second World War was there further council house-building and only after many years of restructuring in the local economy did the private sector begin to play a part again, almost exclusively for owner occupation. The years after 1945 in fact witnessed the final phase of the Rhondda's decline, although this and the more recent beginnings of the community's revival are outside the scope of this study.

---

[1] J.R. and U.K. Hicks, *The incidence of local rates in Great Britain* (Cambridge, 1945), p. 58.

10

Conclusions

This study has examined the development of housing in the Rhondda over a century and a half, drawing where necessary on broader Welsh and British contexts, especially when considering the impact of movements concerned with public health and housing and the legislation that followed. Within the period we have seen the extremes of growth and decline in terms of population changes, the demand for housing, the extent of investment by different agencies, and the impact of such changes on the people.

While the evidence has been presented in a broadly chronological fashion the structure adopted had been one of convenience. The divisions between the periods of time used, for instance, are marked by significant occurrences relevant to the Rhondda's overall development (e.g. the first major attempts to mine coal and the cessation of building before the Great War), and should not be taken as necessarily defining the main phases of the Rhondda's housing development. Instead we must consider a variety of perspectives that relate specifically to housing, namely Rhondda's economic development, the broader political context, housing demand and investment, the agencies of housing provision, and house design.

E.D. Lewis noted that the development of coal working in the lower Rhondda in the period from 1809 to about 1850 represented the beginning of the shift from agriculture.[1] The main phase of colliery development then started in earnest with rapid and continuous growth, from 1850 in Rhondda Fawr and from 1857 in Rhondda Fach, up to 1914. Whilst there was a brief boom in the Rhondda after the Great War (lasting to 1924), the subsequent period is one of economic blight, with no sign of restructuring until at least the mid-1930s (with the passing of new legislation to assist depressed areas). Even then the new jobs were in manufacturing and were mostly located outside the Rhondda.

Phases of economic development based on Lewis's work indicate periods that correspond closely to those of population growth and decline or, more accurately, to the periods of net inmigration and outmigration. In the broader

---

[1] Lewis, *Rhondda Valleys*, pp. 36ff.

political context we can take account of the phases suggested by Byrne.[1] These describe the nature of class relations in Britain but, given the clear social structure in the Rhondda (with a poorly developed middle class), are particularly relevant. Byrne's phases relate to the period from 1835 to 1890 and thence to 1945. The first period (one of 'bourgeois democracy') he sees as being dominated by the capitalist class, with a transition from 1890 towards 'mass democracy', which emerged as a result of a rise in the power and influence of first 'liberal' reformists and then an organised labour movement.

The tensions that arose as a result of the reduction of power of the capitalist class (as far as administrative institutions are concerned) may have intensified the struggles between colliery owner and worker. Whilst the capitalist classes nationally would, for instance, have felt threatened by the working classes, such threats were greater in the Rhondda due to the increasing economic problems faced by the coal industry. Not only were the pits having to work more difficult seams but they were less mechanised than other coalfields and, after the Great War, were facing tough competition from vastly more efficient coalfields in Europe.[2]

Unrest on the part of the workers was, therefore, inevitable in the face of the loss of earnings that resulted from lower tonnages of coal being mined and the attempts by the mine owners to keep wage levels low in order to be more competitive. Organised labour movements in the Rhondda were destined to thrive and the conflict with the capitalist class was dramatically heightened (Chapter 8).

With regard to housing demand and investment, we see half a century of high demand with high investment following a short transitional period as the Rhondda emerged from its rural past. The length of this period should not detract from a cyclical component in the Rhondda's house-building but serves to emphasise the attractiveness of the area for longer-term investment by individuals, speculative builders, institutions and others. Hence a speculative builder could develop more confidently than elsewhere, with houses frequently being occupied before they were properly completed and before services were connected.

Burnett points to the vulnerability of speculative builders as peculiarly subject to fluctuations in the cost of materials, nearly always bought on credit, and because the actual construction of houses, which was by nature a lengthy and somewhat incalculable process, could mean completions

---

[1] Byrne, 'Class', p. 66.
[2] Page-Arnot, *The miners*, p. 528.

appearing on the market at inappropriate times.[1] He also notes that local population and migration factors were usually more powerful determinants than material and labour costs and minor variations in rents. Such factors in the Rhondda clearly helped speculative builders to survive and to avoid the bankruptcies common elsewhere, often resulting from 'unrealistic hopes nurtured in boom times, abetted by easy access to credit and often doomed by under-pricing of work'.[2]

Speculative builders in the Rhondda had, it seems, no difficulty in raising money for their enterprises and found ready buyers after the work was completed. Such a demand is one factor that led directly to an increase in the proportion of owner-occupied property, which exceeded 50 per cent in many parts of the Rhondda in 1914,[3] whereas in other areas builders were more inclined to rent out their property, especially at times when demand was slack. Furthermore, throughout the period (with the possible exception of the Boer War years from 1899 to 1902) members of building clubs were able to raise mortgages and loans collectively (to enable building work to start) or individually (to enable the winding up of the club).

Housing demand remained high during the short post-war boom up to 1924, although building by private investors had all but stopped on account of the economic and political factors discussed in Chapter 8. A substantial housing need, nevertheless, continued throughout the inter-war period until a new balance was restored as a consequence of outmigration and public health action (e.g. closing unfit accommodation and cellar dwellings). The years from 1914 to 1940 in the Rhondda were marked by low investment and falling demand.

The phases relating to the agencies of housing provision are essentially concerned with those providers who predominated at certain times. The boundaries between the phases reflect transitions that may have lasted a decade or more. It should be noted that subsidiary roles were, in any case, retained by some providers in periods dominated by others.

In the earliest, 'farming', phase the more substantial dwellings were provided by the great estates, the humbler cottages mostly being makeshift structures built by their occupants. The beginnings of industrial growth brought the intervention of colliery companies to provide housing for the flood of inmigrant workers, as for instance, with the provision of houses in Dinas by the Rhondda's first major exploiter of coal, Walter Coffin, and some of those who followed (notably David Davies in Ton Pentre, Archibald

---

[1] Burnett, *Social history*, pp. 16–17.
[2] Powell, *Economic history*, p. 73.
[3] Daunton, *Coal metropolis*, p. 108.

Hood in Llwynypia and David Davis in Ferndale). Whilst some housing, even in this early period, was built by other agencies the companies dominated—this being arguably necessary on account of the rurality of much of the Rhondda at that time.[1]

From the 1880s, with the greater availability of loans for building, the private developer and the building club came to thrive. In a minority of cases the colliery companies continued to build both for reasons of investment and, occasionally, philanthropy. The private developers and, to a lesser extent, the building clubs remained the primary agencies of provision until the years immediately preceding the Great War, when the emphasis shifted to the local council (Chapter 5 and 6). Council housing became the major form of housing provision in the inter-war years, although over the twenty years between 1919 and 1939 fewer overall houses were built than in each single year between 1901 and 1914.

Finally we must look at the changes in house design. For the early period C.G. Powell identified two forms, 'small' housing and 'mass' housing, the latter relating in early industrial workings and, in housing terms, indicating a break with the rural past.[2] The advent of such mass housing—essentially dwellings built in terraces—set a pattern for the ensuing 70 years.

To begin with, mass housing had some similarities with the cottages that preceded it. The houses were built using local materials, were simple in style and offered limited accommodation—perhaps two-up and two-down. Many of the similarities were to disappear in the 1860s with increases in house size, more complicated room layouts and greater uniformity. There was increasing use of standardised materials (notably windows, doors, roof timbers, lintels etc). By 1875 the vast majority of dwellings had narrow fronts, two storeys and floor areas of some 500–550 sq.ft.[3] Powell's evidence, from a survey of 50 properties, is reinforced in this study: the earlier properties (e.g. 32 Mary Street, Porth, or 19 Ton Row, Ton Pentre) were generally below 600 sq.ft in size, whereas those built in the 1880s (e.g. 31 Hillside Terrace, Wattstown, or 3 Redfield Street, Ystrad) fell within the 600–700 sq.ft range.

The themes of 'standardisation' and 'uniformity' were further promoted by the adoption of byelaws regarding street layout and building design in

---

[1] This also conforms to the model suggested by Jones, *Colliery settlement*, pp. 32ff.

[2] Powell, 'Occupation and Forms'.

[3] J.B. Lowe and C.G. Powell, 'Fieldwork studies of housing quality in the South Wales coalfield, 1790–1914' (Unpublished paper presented to a symposium on industrial colonies, settlements and planned communities, Aston University, 1974). This work involved a 10% sample survey of 500 properties in the Rhondda built before 1875. The floor areas of these houses were significantly higher than that of houses in ironmaking towns.

1879. This represented, in the Rhondda, the beginning of a third phase, which was undoubtedly the most important and saw the building of nearly 20,000 houses. The byelaws, however, were responsible for much of the Rhondda's worst housing, including cellar dwellings and thousands of homes with basements (Chapter 6). The impact of this phase is still clear in the long, uniform single-fronted terraces, built to almost identical styles and layouts. The typical Rhondda house is of this period and several have been surveyed as part of this study. The property is invariably terraced and would have been built, in most cases, by a private developer or building club. The layout of the house would be such that it is entered via a 'half-hall' giving access to the front room (parlour) and a living room plus single-storey scullery extension. At the end of the half-hall and adjacent to the living room door is the staircase, tightly curved at the top, giving access to a small landing and three bedrooms. A closet and coal store are provided in the back yard. Space standards are generally higher than earlier decades, often approaching 800 sq.ft.

Walls and ground floors would be of locally quarried Pennant sandstone and the floors laid with sandstone flags without any damp proof course. The walls would be built using dressed stone (rock face 'shoddies') to the front with an inner face of random rubble which would then be plastered.[1] Side and rear walls would be of random rubble, sometimes rendered. Inner and outer walls would be 'tied', by conscientious builders, using 'through' stones every yard, the gaps being filled with rubble and lime mortar. Damp proof courses in the walls would normally comprise a double course of slates. Whilst the floor to the half-hall, living room and scullery had stone flags, the front room would often have a suspended wooden floor, supported by joists and 'dwarf' walls, ventilated via air-bricks in the outer wall. Foundations would normally comprise large stones, although later terraces used concrete.

While stone would be used for walls and floors, bricks would be used for chimneys, quoins and door and window openings. Despite the availability of bricks from local collieries these were considered of inferior quality and not used for house building. The Glamorgan ('Scotch') Colliery at Llwynypia, for example, had a sizeable brickworks using clay mined underground in association with coal seams but the bricks were used underground. Bricks for general purpose building were instead obtained from works at Gadlys (Aberdare), Coedely (Tonyrefail) and elsewhere, although a better quality brick would be used for chimneys. Partitions would be brick noggin (i.e. a

---

[1] Shoddies were best obtained from older (and therefore deeper) quarries and were available in different sizes summing to 9in. (e.g. 3in. + 6in.; 4in. + 5in.) so that they might be knitted in with brick quoins, window openings etc. A shoddie would have one faced dressed, but depth and shape would vary.

wooden framework with brick infill) downstairs and lath and plaster upstairs. Ceilings would be lath and plaster throughout.

Windows and doors were made locally in carpenters' shops. The standard window style was a single sash comprising four panes. With bedroom windows the carpenter would leave beading loose so that the housewife could remove the lower sash for cleaning. All windows would be in brick openings headed by flat arches. Roofs would be covered by Welsh slates, the most popular size being the 'Kings' (24in. × 14in.). There would be no eaves.[1] Gutters and downpipes were made of cast iron and would be bought in (e.g. from Coalbrookdale, Shropshire), with brackets made by local blacksmiths.

Decorations or embellishments might most commonly include a ground-floor Venetian window or, possibly, a bay of wood or stone. Other features might include a porch with ornamental tiles (the porch being created by setting the front door a few feet back within the hallway), iron railings around a small garden area to the front, carved pieces on windows, barge boards etc, and patterned crest tiles on roofs. Additional facilities internally would, in the better houses, include a more extensive range for cooking and heating and fireplaces in most rooms.

Some privacy was afforded, it should be noted, by the fact that dwellings tended to have their own back extensions (as opposed to being 'paired' with the adjoining property). This meant that front doors were separated and each house had a back yard not fully visible to the neighbours. This design persisted, despite the higher costs arising from separate chimneys, with no commensurate saving on party walls.

In the Rhondda, as in other parts of Britain, it was a wish of the people for their homes to emulate at least some of the features of dwellings occupied by the middle classes. Within the area's outwardly uniform towns and villages, therefore, marked social hierarchies can be identified, not so much by the house types, but by additional features such as bay windows and front gardens, or even street names. Names such as 'Brynhyfryd' (Beautiful Hill) or 'The Parade' invariable reflect a higher status street.

In design terms the inter-war period is of particular note on account of the impact of garden city ideas promoted strongly by various organisations (including several in Wales) and initially supported by central government through housing legislation from 1890. The key features of garden city type dwellings included lower building densities, better space standards, the provision of bathrooms etc, and had an impact on both council and private

---

[1] Earlier properties would have no soffit or fascia boards. Many later properties had soffits and fascias at the front but just a fascia at the back.

housing. In the Rhondda, however, because of the lack of private development, the impact was essentially confined to council housing and was substantially compromised as the level of government subsidy was reduced (Chapter 3). Space standards in the smaller council dwellings were little different from many of the better properties built by private speculators and building clubs between 1900 and 1914.

Regardless of the perspective taken, there are clear phases in the development of housing in the Rhondda. Whilst some phases relate to national factors, local influences were more important in giving the district a uniqueness that is reflected in its housing. Of particular interest is the role of the building clubs, which in the Valleys continued long after such organisations had disappeared from the rest of Britain. Clubs reflected a collective willingness on the part of working people to raise money to provide a solution to their own housing problems.

The high historical level of owner occupation in the Rhondda is also remarkable, especially in view of the lack in this period of any tax relief on interest payments or inflation to reduce the real cost of repayments. The phenomenon is explained by a unique mix of factors, including the withdrawal of the colliery companies from the housing market; the tendency of private developers to build for sale rather than rent; the relatively high income levels of local miners; the sense of community solidarity and collaboration that helped foster the formation of building clubs; and the absence of a well developed middle class who might have invested more in housing for rent.

Finally, the impact of the collapse of the private housing market, just before the Great War, must be emphasised. The era of the typical Rhondda terraced house was, with few exceptions, to finish as quickly as it had begun (Chapter 6). Building rates decreased from an average of 555 dwellings per year (between 1880 and 1914) to a meagre 21 per year as the Rhondda fell into a dramatic spiral of decline. No other measure could so clearly indicate the way in which the extremes of growth and decline had an influence on the Rhondda's houses, and the lives of the people who lived in them.

Appendix 1: Colliery Housing Developments in the Rhondda

Abergorki Colliery Co.: Cottages, Cwmorki (including 1–11, Upper Row, Treorchy).

Bute Coal Co.: Houses at Old Bute Row and Dumfries Street, Treherbert.

Cambrian Colliery Co.: Bush Houses, Blaenclydach (50).

Coedcae Colliery Co.: Cottages, Coedcae (80).

Walter Coffin: Houses, Dinas (*c.* 50).

Cymmer Colliery Co.: Cottages, Cymmer.

D. Davis & Sons: Huts at Mountain Row and Baptist Row (55); Houses at Long Row, Mountain Row, Baptist Row and George Street, Blaenllechau; Oak Street, Ferndale and Middle Terrace, Stanleytown (*c.* 200).

Dinas Colliery Co.: Concrete houses, Dinas (64).

Dunraven Colliery: Huts (16), Blaenrhondda; Blaenycwm and Brynwyndham Terraces, Tŷnewydd.

Glamorgan Colliery Co.: Amelia, Argyle, Ayton, Cambrian, Campbell, De Winton, Glandwr, Glamorgan, Grange, Holyrood, Inverleith, Llewellyn and Rosedale Terraces, Llwynypia (the 'Scotch' Terraces) (*c.* 300).

Glenavon Garw Colliery: Michael's Road, Blaenycwm (12).

Hafod Colliery Co.: Cottages known as 'Fair Oak', Trehafod.

Lewis' Navigation Coal Co. (later Lewis Merthyr Consolidated Collieries): Houses at Lewis, Gethin and Nythbran Terraces, Llwyncelyn (214).

Lockett's Merthyr Steam Coal Co.: Cottages, Maerdy (20).

London & South Wales Colliery Co.: Caroline Street, Blaenrhondda (51).

Maerdy Colliery Co.: Houses, Maerdy (53).

National Steam Co.: Hillside Terrace, Bailey Street, Lower Bailey Street, Pleasant View, Wattstown (*c.* 140).

Ocean Coal Co.: Houses at Park Road, Cwmparc, Ton Row and Parry Street, Ton Pentre; Glynrhondda Street and Bute Street, Treorchy (*c.* 200).

Pentre Colliery Co.: Cottages, Pentre.

Rhondda Merthyr Colliery Co.: Houses at Victoria and Windsor Streets, Tŷnewydd.

South Wales Coal Co.: Houses at Caroline Street, Blaenrhondda (80).

H. Tylor & Co.: Houses at East Road, Hendrefadog, and North Cross Street, Tylorstown (*c.* 100).

Ynyshir Steam Coal Co.: Houses at James Street and Whitting Street, Ynyshir.

Appendix 2: Building Club Developments in the Rhondda

The figures following the name of the club are the number of dwellings included in the plans submitted; there may be some duplication where modified plans were resubmitted by the same club and it is not always possible to identify the applicants as a building club. The list thus almost certainly understates the role of the clubs.

The source for each entry is given in brackets: CB (Crawshay Bailey estate records); HR (J.H. Richards, Thesis); R (Records of Rhondda Urban District Council); Y (Records of Ystradyfodog Urban Sanitary Authority); YU (Records of Ystradyfodog Urban District Council).

1880: Maerdy Building Society 29 (Y).

1883: Aberaman BC (Pontygwaith) 30 (Y); Ferndale BC (Elm Street) 32 (Y); Rhondda Inn BC (Union Street, Ferndale) 20 (Y).

1884: Clydach Vale BC 40 (Y); Duffryn BC (Ferndale) 23 (Y); Ystrad BC (Redfield Street) 26 (Y) (CB); Messrs Thomas, Morris, Davies, Llewellyn and Rees (Pontygwaith) 15 (Y) (?).

1886: Ystrad BC (Ystrad Terrace) 19 (CB).

1887: Ton BC 15 (Y); 2nd Ystrad BC (Railway Terrace) 19 (CB).

1888: Maxwell BC (Ferndale) 36 (Y); Pentre BC (Queen Street) 13 (Y); Rhondda BC (Ferndale) 40 (Y); Tŷ Isaf BC (Ystrad) 11 (Y).

1889: Dunraven BC 12 (Y) (HR); Pleasant View BC (Tylorstown) 12 (Y) (HR); Messrs Jones, Lloyd, Morgan and Evans (Ystrad) 15 (Y) (?).

1890: Brynheulog BC (Tylorstown) 31 (Y) (HR); Cambrian BC 56 (Y) (HR); Dunraven BC (Primrose Hill, Tonypandy) 10 (HR); Llwynypia BC (Pontrhondda) 31 (Y) (HR); Maerdy BC 15 (Y) (HR); Maerdy BC 7 (Y); Maerdy New Building Society 28 (Y) (HR); Maerdy Royal Building Society 28 (Y); Pentre BC 14 (HR); Penygraig and Dunraven BC (Penygraig) 21 (Y) (HR); Messrs Williams, Jones, Williams and Cox (Trehafod) (Y) (?).

1891: Duffryn Hotel BC 20 (HR); Graig Ynyshir BC 8 (Y); Maerdy BC (Griffiths Street) (Y); North Street BC (Ferndale) 31 (Y); Ynyswen BC (Treorchy) 20 (Y);

Messrs Rees, Simon, Dunn, James, Bumford, Evans, Bruce, Meredith and Rees (Cwmparc) 15 (Y) (?).

1892: Arfryn BC (Tylorstown) 25 (Y); Bodringallt BC 28 (Y) (HR); Bryn Terrace BC (Tylorstown) 17 (Y) (HR); Gellidawel BC (Ystrad) 30 (Y) (HR); Gobaith BC (Tylorstown) 23 (Y) (HR); Libanus BC (Treherbert) 30 (Y) (HR); Pentre Building Society 13 (Y) (HR); Pentre BC 11 (HR); Porth BC (Llethrddu Road) 11 (Y); Treorky Building Society 38 (Y) (HR); Mr Willis and others (Gelli) 22 (Y) (?).

1893: Bwllfa and Gelli BC 52 (HR); Ferndale BC (Duffryn Street) 13 (Y); Gwernllwyn BC (Tylorstown) 30 (Y) (HR); Penrhys Isaf BC (Pontygwaith) 25 (Y) (HR); Pontygwaith 2nd Workmens' BC (Llewellyn Street) 35 (Y) (HR); Rhondda Terrace BC 42 (HR)

c. 1893: Gelligaled BC 14+ (YU).

1894: Arthur Street BC 24 (HR); Blaenclydach BC 37 (HR); Cwmparc BC 20 (HR); Graig BC 25 (HR); Miskin BC 60 (HR); Partridge BC 25 (HR); Sherwood BC 30 (HR); Stanley BC 80 (HR); Trealaw BC 30 (HR); Tŷnewydd BC 52 (HR); Tyntilla BC 30 (HR).

1895: Bwllfa and Gelli BC 56 (HR); Glamorgan BC 20 (HR); Glynrhydynog BC 19 (HR) (YU); Maerdy BC 111 (HR); Pleasant View Extension BC 13 (HR); Robert Street BC 13 (HR); Ynysgau BC 20 (HR).

1896: Baglan BC 19 (HR); Queens Hotel BC 20 (HR); Wattstown BC 25 (HR).

1897: Hafod BC 24 (HR) (YU); Trealaw BC 50 (HR).

1901: Greenfield BC 15 (HR); Ynyscynon BC 14 (HR); New Century BC 26 (HR) (R); Pontrhondda BC 12 (HR); York BC 11 (HR).

1902: Maesffrwd BC 18 (HR); Maindy BC 14 (HR); New Century BC 13 (HR) (R).

c. 1902: Blaenrhondda BC (Miskin Street, Treherbert) (R).

1903: Bodringallt BC 17 (HR); Bryngolau BC 41 (HR) (R).

1904: Excelsior BC 13 (HR); Hendrefan BC 55 (HR).

c. 1905: Trealaw Road BC c. 17 (R).

1906: Cymru Fydd BC 62 (HR); Pentre BC 24 (HR); St David's BC 42 (HR).

1907: Alexandra BC 36 (HR); Ardwyn BC 61 (HR); Ffynnon Wen BC 26 (HR); Margaret Street BC 57 (HR); Pleasant View and Brynawel BC (Ynyshir) 60 (HR) (R); Woodlands BC 50 (HR); Ynysfaelog No 1 BC 92 (HR).

1908: Miskin Manor BC 16 (HR); Tŷnycymmer BC 68 (HR); Witherdene BC 12 (HR); Ynyswen BC 22 (HR).

1909: Belgrave BC 55 (HR); Chepstow Road BC 45 (HR); Clifton Road BC 32 (HR); Danygraig BC (Maerdy Road, Maerdy) 100 (HR) (R); Heath BC 30 (HR); Llyn Crescent BC (Ferndale) 13 (CB); Miskin Manor BC 16 (HR); Pantyreistedd BC 12 (HR); Turberville BC 34 (HR); Tŷnycae BC 28 (HR); Wattstown BC 51 (HR).

1910: Bronllwyn Road BC 58 (HR); Ferndale BC 56 (HR); Hendrecafn BC 30 (HR); Stanley BC 34 (HR); Turberville BC 11 (HR); BC (Kennard Street, Gelli) (CB) (?); BC (Pleasant View, Wattstown) 24 (CB) (?).

1911: Coronation BC 30 (HR); Penrhyn BC 27 (HR); Wattstown BC 17 (HR).

1913: Penrhys Isaf BC 22 (HR) (CB).

1914: Crawshay BC 25 (HR); Excelsior BC 48 (HR); Garth Crescent BC 41 (HR).

Appendix 3: Council Housing Developments in the Rhondda before the Second World War

1920: Maerdy (15 dwellings): Steel Huts at Maerdy Park. Completed Summer 1920, demolished 1930.

1921: Penygraig (44 dwellings): Bransby Street, Millbourne Street, Aubrey Road. Completed from Autumn 1921.

1921–2: Section 12(3) houses (39 dwellings): Eileen Place, Treherbert; Taff Street, Treherbert; Tyntyla Avenue, Ystrad; Crawshay Road, Penygraig; Mikado Street, Penygraig; Llanfair Road, Penygraig. Completed from end of 1921.

1924: Ferndale (50 dwellings): Highfield. Completed from end of 1924.

1926: Wattstown (111 dwellings): Bryn Terrace, Cefn Road, Pleasant View, Heol y Twyn, Heol Llechau, Heol Ceiriog. Completed from end of 1926.

1936: Gelli (20 dwellings): King Street. Completed autumn 1936.

1937: Llwynypia (27 dwellings): Church Street, William Street, Mountain View. Completed spring 1937.

The council also acquired other dwellings through repossession after loans issued under the 1899 Small Dwellings Acquisition Act were not repaid. Some of these were sold but others were retained for letting.

Bibliography

Archival Sources (all at the Glamorgan Record Office, Cardiff)

Ystradyfodwg Local Board, Urban Sanitary Authority and Urban District Council: Minutes; Byelaws; Annual Reports of the Medical Officer of Health.
Rhondda Urban District Council: Minutes; Annual Reports of the Medical Officer of Health.
Records of the Victoria Building Club, Caerphilly.

Official Publications

Reports of the Commissioners of Inquiry into the state of education in Wales (Parliamentary Papers, 1847, XXVII).
Report of the Committee appointed to enquire into and report upon ... the cost of living to the working classes ... which may have arisen under war conditions (Cd 8980, 1918).
Report of the Committee ... to consider questions of building construction with the provision of dwellings for the working classes ... etc (Cd 9191, 1918).
Report of the Committee appointed ... to consider the position of the building industry after the war (Cd 9197, 1918).
Report of the Departmental Committee on Building Byelaws (Cd 9213, 1918).
Report of the Departmental Committee on Building Byelaws, Minutes of Evidence (Cd 9214, 1918).
Ministry of Health, *Report of the South Wales Regional Survey Committee* (1920).

Other Published Works and Theses

'Public utility societies in Wales', *Welsh Housing Yearbook* (1916), 58–60.
'1926 remembered and revealed', *Llafur*, 2 (1977), 24–5.
'Housing and industrial unrest', *Welsh Housing and Development Yearbook* (1918), 88–9.
'The government's housing scheme', *Welsh Housing and Development Yearbook* (1919), 86–8.
D.H. Aldcroft and P. Fearon (ed.), *British economic fluctuations 1790-1939* (1972).
J. Burnett, *A social history of housing 1815–1970* (1978).
D. Byrne, 'Class and the local state', *International Journal of Urban and Regional Research*, 6 (1982), 61–82.
D.S. Byrne et al., *Housing and health: the relationship between housing conditions and the health of council tenants* (Aldershot, 1986).
E.L. Chappell, 'Individual ownership housing schemes', *Welsh Housing and Development Yearbook* (1923), 89–94.
  'The case for municipal housing', *Welsh Housing and Development Yearbook* (1923), 43–8.
E.A. Charles, 'Activities of local authorities in Wales and Monmouthshire', *Welsh Housing and Development Yearbook* (1928), 87–97.

L.B. Collier, 'A detailed survey of the South Wales coal industry from *c*. 1750 to *c*. 1850' (Unpublished University of London Ph.D. thesis, 1940).
E.G. Culpin, 'What a garden city is', *Welsh Housing Yearbook* (1916), 66–8.
M.J. Daunton, *Coal Metropolis. Cardiff 1870–1914* (Leicester, 1977).
   (Ed.) *Councillors and tenants: local authority housing in English cities 1919–1939* (Leicester, 1984).
   'Miners' houses: South Wales and the Great Northern Coalfield, 1880–1914', *International Review of Social History*, 25 (1980), 143–75.
J. Davies, 'Glamorgan and the Bute Estate, 1766–1947' (Unpublished University of Wales [Aberystwyth] Ph.D. thesis, 1969).
   'The end of the great estates and the rise of freehold farming in Wales', *Welsh History Review*, 7 (1974), 186–212.
   Cardiff and the Marquesses of Bute (Cardiff, 1981).
J.R. Davies, 'Brynwyndham village, upper Rhondda Fawr', *Morgannwg*, 20 (1976), 53–65.
P.R. Davies, *Historic Rhondda: an archaeological and topographical survey, 800 BC – AD 1850* (Treorchy, 1989).
M. Doughty (ed.), *Building the industrial city* (Leicester, 1986).
D. Egan, *Coal society: a history of the South Wales mining valleys 1840-1980* (Llandysul, 1987).
M.W. Flinn (ed.), *Report on the sanitary condition of the labouring population of Great Britain by Edwin Chadwick, 1842* (Edinburgh, 1965).
E. Gauldie, *Cruel habitations: a history of working-class housing 1780–1918* (1974).
J. Ginswick (ed.), *Labour and the poor in England and Wales, 1849–1851. 3. South Wales and North Wales* (1983).
C.E. Gwyther, 'Sidelights on religion and politics in the Rhondda Valley', *Llafur*, 3 (1980), 30–43.
J.R. and U.K. Hicks, *The incidence of local rates in Great Britain* (Cambridge, 1945).
A.K. Hignell, 'Suburban development in north Cardiff 1850–1919: a case study of the patterns and processes of growth in the parishes of Llanishen, Lisvane and Whitchurch' (Unpublished University of Wales [Cardiff] Ph.D. thesis, 1987).
P. Jeremy, 'Life on Circular 703: the crisis of destitution in the South Wales coalfield during the lockout of 1926', *Llafur*, 2 (1977), 65–75.
H.S. Jevons, *The British coal trade* (Repr. Newton Abbot, 1969).
B.D. Jones, *Early history of the Rhondda Valley. Baptist centenary, 1810–1910* (Pontypridd, 1910).
P.N. Jones 'Aspects of the population and settlement geography of the South Wales coalfield 1850–1926' (Unpublished University of Birmingham Ph.D. thesis, 1965).
   Colliery Settlement in the South Wales coalfield, 1850 to 1926 (Hull, 1969).
S.R. Jones and J.T. Smith, 'The Houses of Breconshire. Part 1: The Builth District', *Brycheiniog*, 9 (1963), 1–77.
   'The Houses of Breconshire. Part 6: The Faenor and Penderyn District', *Brycheiniog*, 16 (1988), 1–37.
E.D. Lewis, *The Rhondda Valleys* (2nd ed., Cardiff, 1984).
J.A. Lovat-Fraser, 'What town planning means', *Welsh Housing Yearbook* (1916), 36–8.
J. Lowe, *Welsh industrial workers' housing, 1775–1875* (Cardiff, 1977).
J.B. Lowe and C.G. Powell, 'Fieldwork studies of housing quality in the South Wales coalfield, 1790–1914' (Paper given to a symposium on industrial colonies, settlements and planned communities, University of Aston, Birmingham, 1974).

B.H. Malkin, *The scenery, antiquities and biography of South Wales* (Repr. Wakefield, 1970).
P. Malpass and A. Murie, *Housing policy and practice* (1987).
J. Melling (ed.), *Housing, social policy and the state* (1980).
R. Page-Arnot, *The miners: years of struggle* (1953).
I. Peate, *The Welsh house* (Liverpool, 1946).
'The Long House Again', *Folk Life*, 2 (1964), 76–9.
J.R.E. Phillips, 'Sources of income in a distressed area of south Wales', *Welsh Housing and Development Yearbook* (1936), 47–53.
C.G. Powell, 'Fifty years of progress', *Built Environment*, (Oct. 1974), 532–5.
An economic history of the British building industry 1815–1979 (1982).
Rhondda Borough Council, *Rhondda District Plan. Report 1. Population*.
J.H. Richards, 'Fluctuations in house building in the south Wales coalfield 1851–1954' (Unpublished University of Wales [Cardiff] M.A. thesis, 1956).
'The demographic factor' in H. Richards (ed.), *Population and factor movements in economic development* (Cardiff, 1976).
J.H. Richards and J.P. Lewis, 'House building in the South Wales coalfield, 1851–1913' in W.E. Minchinton (ed.) *Industrial South Wales 1750–1914: essays in Welsh economic history* (1969), 235–48.
T. Richards, 'The improvement of colliery districts', *Welsh Housing Yearbook* (1917), 76–80.
W.J. Roberts, 'Housing after the war', *Welsh Housing and Development Yearbook* (1917), 82–6.
C.T. Ruthen, 'The town planning movement in Wales', *Welsh Housing and Development Association Yearbook* (1917), 66–74.
P. Smith, *Houses of the Welsh countryside: a study in historical geography* (1975).
M. Swenarton, *Homes fit for heroes: the politics and architecture of early state housing in Britain* (1981).
W. Thomas, 'War and the housing problem', *Welsh Housing Yearbook* (1916), 62–4.
W. Thompson, *Housing up-to-date* (1907).
C.F. Ward, 'Town planning in the Welsh Valleys', *Welsh Housing Year Book* (1916), 84–8.
S.V. Ward, 'Interwar Britain: a study of government spending, planning and uneven economic development', *Built Environment*, 17 (1981), 96–108.
P. Wilding, 'Towards Exchequer subsidies for housing, 1906–1914', *Social and Economic Administration*, 6 (1972), 3–18.
E. Wiliam, *Home-made homes: dwellings of the rural poor in Wales* (Cardiff, 1988).
H. Williams, *Davies the Ocean: railway king and coal tycoon* (Cardiff, 1991).
J. Williams, *Digest of Welsh historical statistics* (Cardiff, 1985).
L.J. Williams, 'The road to Tonypandy', *Llafur*, 1 (1970), 3–14.
M.I. Williams, 'A general view of Glamorgan houses and their interiors in the seventeenth and eighteenth centuries', *Glamorgan Historian*, 10 (1974), 157–76.
N. Williams, *A history of Blaenllechau School* (Ferndale, 1979).
W. Williams, *A sanitary survey of Glamorganshire* (Cardiff, 1895).

Index

Abercarn, Mon. 33
Aberdare 8, 30, 35
Abergorki Colliery Co. 40
Abergwynfi Building Club 51
Abersychan, Mon. 48, 99
Abertillery, Mon. 99
Abraham, William, MP 88
America Fach 20

Bailey, Crawshay: *see* Crawshay Bailey estate
Blaenavon, Mon. 8
Blaenclydach 38, 80, 81, 83, 109, 110
Blaenllechau 14–16, 24, 38, 39, 42, 45, 63, 64, 69, 72, 77
Blaenrhondda 33, 38, 40, 41, 47, 70, 73, 77, 80, 110
Blaenycwm 25, 28, 33, 38, 39, 70, 80–1, 104, 109
brickworks 116
Bristol & West of England Building Society 49
Brown, Thomas Owen 59
Brownstown 59
Brynwyndham 33, 34
building clubs 48–56, 90–1, 104, 118, 1202,

building cycles 84–5
building materials 11, 12, 20, 91, 103, 116–17
building societies 49
Burnett, J. 113
Burnyeat Brown & Co. 32
Bute estate 12, 14, 19, 20, 23–4, 32
Bute Merthyr Colliery 20
Butetown (Rhymney) 33
Butler, John 53
Byelaws (Public Health Act 1875) 37, 86, 79, 99–100, 116
Byrne, D. 8, 113

Caerphilly 49–50, 94
Cambrian Combine 45, 80, 88, 92, 105
Cardiff 32, 48
Carmichael Committee 91
cellar dwellings 57, 63–7, 108, 116
Chadwick, Edwin 9, 31
Chappell, E.L. 103
Clydach Vale 45, 63, 65, 76, 80, 110
Clyngwyn 33
Cobden, Richard 12

Coedely 116
Coffin, Walter 19, 23, 24, 39, 114
colliery company housing 19–20, 24, 30, 39–47, 119–20
council housing 84, 93–111, 122
Crawshay Bailey estate 19, 23, 25, 25–30, 32, 40–2, 53–5, 105
Cule, Evan 36
Culpin, E.G. 83, 95
Cwmgorki 40
Cwmparc 25, 27, 38, 39, 80, 110
Cwmsaerbren 20
Cymmer 12–14, 20, 21, 23, 38, 79
Cymmer Colliery Co. 45
Cymru Fydd Building Club 56

Daunton, M.J. 85
Davies, David, 1st Lord Davies 25, 30, 39, 53, 95, 114
John 53
Thomas 36
Walter 12
Davis, D. & Son 42, 45, 115
death rate 35, 80, 78–9
Dinas 7, 19, 20, 22, 23, 24, 38, 39, 42, 71, 77, 79, 81, 109, 115
Dinas Steam Colliery Co. 42–5
Dunraven Collieries 24, 40
Dunraven estate 23, 33

Eirw 20
Evans, John William 55

farming, decline of 23–4
Ferndale 38, 39, 40, 42, 53, 54, 55, 59, 61, 67, 72, 78, 105, 115
Ferndale Coal Co. 45
Ferndale Colliery Co. 80
Ferndale Gas Co. 35
Fernhill 24, 38, 77, 80, 95
Finance Act (1910) 87
Flinn, M.W. 32

Gadlys (Aberdare) 116
garden city movement 83, 84, 93–4, 117–18
Gelli 59, 60, 67, 108
General Strike (1926) 105
Gilfach Goch 95
Glamorgan Coal Co. 47
Glamorgan Colliery Co. 80
Glamorgan County Council 75

126

INDEX

Glamorgan (Scotch) Colliery 30, 116
Glenavon Garw Collieries 104
Graig Ddu 20
Griffiths, William 53
Gyfeillon 20

Hadley, Leonard 19
Hall, Benjamin 33
Hendreforgan 95
Hicks, J.R. and U.K. 111
Hood, Archibald 30, 39, 114–15
house layouts 42, 32, 24–5, 30
house sizes 20, 115–16, 118
housing, pre-industrial 11–18
Housing Acts (1890–1923) 79–80, 83, 92, 97, 100
housing cycles 48
housing finance 55, 85–7, 91–2, 104, 106 7
Housing Reform Co. 94, 95
Howell, Abraham 25
Hughes, Hugh Thomas 55

industrial relations and housing 87–9, 103, 105–6
Insole, George 20
investment in housing, private 57–63, 83–4, 90

James, D.W. 19
  John 59
Jenkins, John 53, 55
  Thomas 53
  William 53
Jevons, H.S. 40, 48–9, 56, 94, 95
Johnson, Richard 33
Jones, David 36
  Edward 53
  Jenkin 55
  S.R. 16
Joseph, Thomas 33

labour costs and housing 86, 103
land, price of 86
Lewis, E.D. 7, 112
Lewis Merthyr Consolidated Collieries Ltd 45
lighting 35
Llantrisant parish 7
Llanwonno parish 7
Llewellyn, Obadiah 53
  Rees 53
Llwyncelyn 40, 45, 46
Llwynypia 30, 31, 38, 39, 42–5, 47, 59, 62, 73, 76, 80, 109, 116
London & South Wales Co. 33
Low, Bruce 75

Maerdy 73, 96–7, 100–1, 106
Maerdy Colliery 40
Malkin, B.H. 11
Merthyr Tydfil 8, 9, 30, 35, 49, 94
Meyrick, Mary Jane 55
  William 53
model dwellings 33
Morgan, Joseph 25
  William 53

National Colliery Co. 80
National Housing Reform Council 84
National Steam Coal Co. 42
New Lanark, Lanarkshire 33

Ocean Colliery Co. 25, 30, 39, 80, 95, 110
overcrowding 107
Owen, Robert 33
owner occupation 118

Page-Arnot, R. 89, 103
Penderyn, Brecs. 16
Penrhiwfer 80
Pentre 38, 79
Pentre & District Trades & Labour Council 67
Pentre Building Club 51
Penygefnen 20, 22, 23
Penygraig 14, 38, 84, 88, 96–7, 98, 100–1, 105, 109, 110
Penyrenglyn 11, 36
Pont Neath Vechan 11
Pontardawe 99
Pontygwaith 11, 80, 110
Pontypridd 11
Pontypridd, Llantrisant & Rhondda Valleys Benefit Building Society 49
Pontypridd Poor Law Union 106
Pontypridd & Rhondda Valleys Master Builders' Association 97, 103
Pontypridd Water Co. 35, 76, 79, 80, 81
Pope, William 36
population growth and decline of 7–8, 10, 19–20
Porth 16, 19, 20, 25, 26, 38, 115
Powell, C.G. 20, 23, 115
Principality Building Society 109
public health 9, 33–7, 75–82
Public Health Acts (1848–75) 32, 35
public utility societies 94–5, 104
Pugh, W. 97

Reece, Francis Henry 53
Rees, Jonathan 51, 53
refuse disposal 78, 81–2, 109
rents 47, 58, 67, 90–1, 97

INDEX

Rhigos 7
Rhiwbina, Cardiff 94
Rhondda Valley Workmen's Housing Committee 83
Rhys, Watkin 36, 75
Richards, Alban 58
  Evan 53
  J.H. 58, 84–5
Riches, John Osborne 25
Rideout, F.G. 97
Roberts, Benjamin 108
  Esra 25
  W.J. 87

Salt, Titus 33
Saltaire, Yorks. 33
sanitation 30–2, 35–6, 40, 77–8
sewerage 76, 81, 109–110
Shepherd & Evans, Messrs 19
Small Dwellings Acquisition Acts (1899-1919) 55, 90, 104
Smith, J.T. 16
South Dunraven Colliery 47
South Wales Coal Co. 40
South Wales Garden Cities and Town Planning Association 94
speculative builders 57, 59
Stanleytown 45, 79
Store House 20
subsidence 96, 104–5
Sumner Committee 91

Thomas, D.A., 1st Lord Rhondda 92
  Daniel 53
  David 58–9
  J. 97
  Thomas 51, 53
  William 53
  William John 53
Ton Co-Operative Society 68
Ton Pentre 25, 29, 36, 38, 39, 115
Tonypandy 36, 38, 79, 88, 110
Tonyrefail 116
Town Planning Act (1909) 84, 86, 93, 94–5
Trealaw 36, 38, 59, 63–6, 67, 79, 108, 110
Trebanog 7, 38, 80
Trehafod 20, 80

Treherbert 20, 23, 32, 34, 36, 38, 73, 77, 81, 95, 97, 104
Treorchy 32, 36, 38
Troedyrhiw 19, 36
Tudor Walters Report 87, 90, 91, 99
Tylor, H. & Co. 40
Tylorstown 39, 40, 40–2, 43, 59, 71, 79, 80
Tynewydd 33, 38

United National Collieries 45

Vaynor, Brecs. 16
Victoria Building Club, Caerphilly 49–50

wages and housing 89
Walters, Tudor: see Tudor Walters Report
Ward, C.F. 99
  S.C. 106
water supply 35–6, 76–7, 80–1, 110
Wattstown 40, 42, 43, 45, 101, 102, 115
Wattstown Building Club 51
Webb, Thomas 25
Welsh Economic Building Society 42
Welsh Garden Cities Ltd 94, 95
Welsh Housing Association 94
Welsh Housing and Development Association 94, 95, 100, 103–4
Welsh Town Planning and Housing Trust 95, 99, 100, 104
Welsh Town Planning and Housing Trust Ltd 49
White, William 53
Williams, Daniel James 55
  Thomas 59
Williamstown 7, 77

Ynysfeio 39, 77
Ynyshir 19, 38, 79
Ynysybwyl 94
Ystrad 11, 14, 16, 17, 36, 38, 51, 52, 58–9, 67, 69, 81, 115
Ystrad Gas & Water Co. 35, 76–7, 80
Ystradfechan 12
Ystradyfodwg Local Board 75
Ystradyfodwg parish 7–8
Ystradyfodwg Urban District Council 7
Ystradyfodwg Urban Sanitary Authority 7, 35